1st Workshop on Natural Language Processing and Information 2017

Associated with the 11th International Conference on Recent Advances in Natural Language Processing (RANLP 2017)

Varna, Bulgaria
7 September 2017

ISBN: 978-1-5108-5524-3

Printed from e-media with permission by:

Curran Associates, Inc.
57 Morehouse Lane
Red Hook, NY 12571

Printed by Curran Associates, Inc. (2018)

Association for Computational Linguistics
209 N. Eighth Street
Stroudsburg, Pennsylvania 18360

Phone: 1-570-476-8006
Fax: 1-570-476-0860

acl@aclweb.org

Additional copies of this publication are available from:

Curran Associates, Inc.
57 Morehouse Lane
Red Hook, NY 12571 USA
Phone: 845-758-0400
Fax: 845-758-2633
Email: curran@proceedings.com
Web: www.proceedings.com

NLPIR 2017

The 1st Workshop on
Natural Language Processing and Information Retrieval

Proceedings of the Workshop

associated with
The 11th International Conference on
Recent Advances in Natural Language Processing
(RANLP 2017)

Varna, Bulgaria

7 September, 2017

Preface

Welcome to the 1st Workshop on Natural Language Processing and Information Retrieval (NLPIR 2017) in Varna, Bulgaria, 7 September 2017. The Workshop aims to further stimulate research on the use of NLP in information retrieval tasks. It also serves as an interactive platform for researchers to exchange ideas and experiences, discuss difficult and shared problems, and to expand the research area in such a field.

NLPIR 2017 Organizers:

Michael Oakes *(University of Wolverhampton)*

Mireille Makary *(University of Wolverhampton, Lebanese International University)*

Invited Speakers:

Leonidas Tsekouras, *National Centre for Scientific Research "Demokritos"*

Amir Hazem, *University of Nantes*

Preslav Nakov, *Qatar Computing Research Institute, HBKU*

Georgi Karadzhov, Tsvetomila Mihaylova, Pepa Gencheva, *Sofia University*

Victoria Bobicev, *Technical University of Moldova*

Table of Contents

Workshop Programme

September 7, 2017

Session 1

09:00 - 09:40 *N-gram graphs and Entity graphs: from sub-word to entity neighborhoods* **Leonidas Tsekouras**

09:40 – 10:20 *MappSent: a Textual Mapping Approach for Question-to-Question Similarity* **Amir Hazem**

10:30 – 11:00 *Coffee break*

11:00 – 11:50 *Fact Checking in the Post Truth Era* **Preslav Nagov, Georgi Karadjov , Pepa Gencheva and Tsvetomila Mihaylova**

11:50 – 12:30 *What are people searching for?* **Victoria Bobicev**

12:30 – 14:00 *Lunch*

Session 2

14:00 – 14:30 *Deception Detection for the Russian Language: Lexical and Syntactic Parameters* **Dina Pisarevskaya, Tatiana Litvinova and Olga Litvinova**

14:30 – 15:00 *oIQa: An Opinion Influence Oriented Question Answering Framework with Applications to Marketing Domain* **Dumitru-Clementin Cercel, Cristian Onose, Stefan Trausan-Matu and Florin Pop**

15:00- 15:30 *Automatic Summarization of Online Debates* **Nattapong Sanchan, Ahmet Aker and Kalina Bontcheva**

15:30 – 16:00 *Coffee break*

Session 3

16:00- 16:30 *A Game with a Purpose for Automatic Detection of Children's Speech Disabilities using Limited Speech Resources* **Reem Elhady, Mohamed Elmahdy, Injy Hamed and Slim Abdennadher**

Deception Detection for the Russian Language: Lexical and Syntactic Parameters

Dina Pisarevskaya [1], Tatiana Litvinova [2] and Olga Litvinova [2]
1 Institute for Oriental Studies of the RAS, Moscow, Russia
2 RusProfiling Lab, Voronezh State Pedagogical University
dinabpr@gmail.com, centr_rus_yaz@mail.ru

Abstract

The field of automated deception detection in written texts is methodologically challenging. Different linguistic levels (lexics, syntax and semantics) are basically used for different types of English texts to reveal if they are truthful or deceptive. Such parameters as POS tags and POS tags n-grams, punctuation marks, sentiment polarity of words, psycholinguistic features, fragments of syntactic structures are taken into consideration. The importance of different types of parameters was not compared for the Russian language before and should be investigated before moving to complex models and higher levels of linguistic processing. On the example of the Russian Deception Bank Corpus we estimate the impact of three groups of features (POS features including bigrams, sentiment and psycholinguistic features, syntax and readability features) on the successful deception detection and find out that POS features can be used for binary text classification, but the results should be double-checked and, if possible, improved.

1 Introduction

In the contemporary world, we get information from diverse sources: news stories and social media posts, product reviews and online communication. Automated deception detection is the field of natural language processing which studies what methods can be used to separate truth from deception, in written texts and in transcripts of oral communication, by identifying verbal predictors of deception. The influence of Internet communications is growing, therefore identification of deceptive information in short written texts is of vital importance.

Deception can be broadly defined as "the intentional misrepresentation of information", and the forms can be different, from direct lie to exaggeration (Hancock et al., 2007a). It can be also understood as "deliberate attempt to mislead others" (DePaulo et al., 2003). In deceptive texts, the content about the given event's factuality is either hidden from the reader or is "uttered in a way that camouflages the factual side of a given proposition" (Heidari et al., 2017). Human ability to detect deception is slightly above 50% (DePaulo et al., 1997). It highlights the importance of automated deception detection methods.

Most papers dealing with this topic were performed using English texts, but, due to the development of data sets for other languages, automated deception detection was recently taken into consideration for other languages too. The evaluation of truthfulness of the narrative has been commonly understood as a text classification task employing the methods of machine learning, data mining and information retrieval (Zhou et al., 2004; Hirschberg et al., 2005; Fuller et al., 2008; Mihalcea and Strapparava, 2009; Zhang et al., 2009). Techniques for detecting deception in text usually use different levels of language analysis: lexics, syntax, semantics, discourse and pragmatics levels. Studies often focus on lexics and semantics and may add some syntactic, discourse and pragmatics principles. As the field of deception detection is methodologically challenging for different sciences, psycholinguistic markers and psycho-social dictionaries are also used in natural language processing methods and models.

The question of deception detection is important for information retrieval, as it could help search engines to give an indication to the user of how reliable or truthful each retrieved document

Proceedings of Natural Language Processing and Information Retrieval Workshop, pages 1–10,
Varna, Bulgaria, Sep 7 2017.

is. Automated deception detection could be included in search engines page ranking algorithms.

2 Related Work

Problem of automated deception detection in oral communication has been the subject of research interest for a long time. This interdisciplinary field is an interesting issue for computational linguistics, speech processing, psychology (polygraph tests for non-verbal cues and psychological markers for verbal cues), and physiology studies. Written texts are also the subject of research for studying deception detection methods. In general, in regard to the computational linguistics and natural language processing, different tools and software already exist which help in detecting deception and lie.

On the lexics level, psycholinguistic lexicons – for instance, the general-purpose psycho-social dictionary Linguistic Inquiry and Word Count (LIWC) (Pennebaker and Francis, 1999) – can be adapted for binary text classifications. As for records of oral communication, it was revealed, using LIWC software, that people show less negative emotions, use less inconsistencies and modal verbs, use more modificators and speak longer if they tell deceptive information (Ali and Levine, 2008). Three data sets of texts, focused on three different topics (opinions on abortion, opinions on death penalty, and feelings about the best friend), were taken for the experiment on written English (Mihalcea and Strapparava, 2009). The classes of words from LIWC are categories relevant to psychological processes (for example, emotion or cognition), and the saliencies of these classes in truthful and deceptive texts were taken as features. An average classifier demonstrated 70% accuracy rate, showing that good separation between truthful and deceptive texts can be obtained (Mihalcea and Strapparava, 2009). LIWC-based analysis of written computer-mediated communication transcripts showed that deceptive texts use more sense-based words, fewer self-reference pronouns but more other-oriented pronouns (Hancock et al., 2007b). Generally, it was also found out, based on LIWC, that deceptive texts use more negative words, fewer exclusive words (for example, "only" and "just"), but more motion words (Bond and Lee, 2005).

Lexics and semantics analysis levels can be combined. Predictive lexical cues can be taken from the Statement Validity Analysis (Porter and Yuille, 1996). Such markers can be identified and extracted from texts, and with standard classification methods and algorithms (neural networks, decision trees, logistic regression) 74% accuracy can be achieved (Fuller et al., 2009).

As to facts in the described event, in (Sauri and Pustejovsky, 2012) the model is based on grammatical fact description structures in English and kindred languages. It is implemented in De Facto, a factuality profiler for eventualities based on lexical types and syntactic constructions.

Different types of written texts were investigated to find differences between truth and lie. Fake online reviews, fake social network profiles (Kumar and Reddy, 2012), fake dating profiles, fake news reports were already investigated. LIWC can be also used for fake dating profiles detection: motion verbs and words with "but", "except", and "without" should be taken into consideration (Toma and Hancock, 2012).

As concerns deceptive reviews, most of the works about opinion spam detection focus on the textual content of users' reviews by using word-level unigrams or bigrams as features, along with specific lexicons (LIWC, Word-Net Affect (Strapparava and Valitutti, 2004)), to learn classifiers (Li et al., 2013). The special website, which contains tools for manual and automated detection of fake reviews (https://www.cs.uic.edu/~liub/FBS/fake-reviews.html), suggests to analyze such lexical parameters as n-grams, POS tag n-grams, content similarity and style similarity of reviews written by different authors. Ott et al. (2011) archived nearly 90% accuracy using only n-grams as features. Truthful/deceptive texts classification is connected with texts' sentiment: authors of deceptive texts use more emotions, judgements and estimations (Hancock et al., 2011). Therefore, syntactic patterns can be used to distinguish feelings from arguments based on facts, and there are different classes of argumentations styles. Combining n-grams features and syntactic features derived from Probabilistic Context Free Grammar parse trees, model in (Feng et al., 2012) obtained 91.2% accuracy. Support vector machine classification showed 86% accuracy in deceptive reviews detection (negative deceptive opinion spam), also based on lexical and syntactic features (Ott et al., 2013). As to the semantics level of text analysis, the consistency of a text with similar texts is important: for example, how the definite review about the hotel goes with similar texts in the data set. Pairs "attribute-descriptor" are created, and the function of the compatibility scores, based on information from the whole corpus, is counted. The precision is about 91% (Feng and Hirst, 2013). Other approach is to use Lexical Chain Based Semantic Similarity algorithm (99.75% accuracy) (Dewang and Singh, 2017). Some consistency features could also be used (Mukherjee et al., 2016). In (Chen et al., 2015) experiments for three features types are held. Shallow syntactic features include bag-of-words features, punctuation (exclamation and question marks), POS-unigrams and present baseline based on LIWC. POS tags bigrams are considered separately, as they show not only information about POS tags frequencies, but also the structure of the sentence. Connectives frequencies, derived from a shallow discourse parser trained on Penn Discourse Treebank, are used as features on discourse and pragmatics level. Frequencies of positive, negative and negation terms from the sentimental dictionary are used as sentiment features. Precision for explicit discourse classifier is 91.2%; precision for different features combinations classifiers is from 98.1% to 89.4%. So we can conclude that psycholinguistic features, sentiment features, POS tags and POS tags n-grams, punctuation marks, lemmas n-grams are helpful in deception detection on lexical and syntactic levels.

Regarding the next specific deception detection field, fake news detection, we can see that on the lexical level stylistic features (POS tags, length of words, subjectivity terms etc.) can be extracted that help to apart tabloid news (they are similar to fake news) with 77% accuracy (Lex et al., 2010). Numbers, imperatives, names of media persons can be extracted from news headlines (Clark, 2014); the numbers of these keywords can be used as features for classification with SVMs or Naive Bayes Classifier (Lary et al., 2010). In (Hardalov et al., 2016) the combined approach for automatically distinguishing credible from fake news, based on different features and combining different levels, is presented: there are linguistic (n-gram), credibility-related (capitalization, punctuation, pronoun use, sentiment polarity), and semantic (embeddings and DBPedia data) features. The accuracy is from 75% to 99% on three different data sets.

Deception detection studies in criminal analysis showed the importance of stylometric and psychological features, if we speak about verbal cues. Stylometry studies text on the basis of its stylistic features and can be used in order to attribute the text to an author (authorship attribution) or to get information about the author, for example, about her/his gender or personality (author profiling) (Fornaciari and Poesio, 2013). It is based on extracting low-level verbal cues from large amounts of text. Features in stylometric analysis can be surface-related (frequencies of function words, frequencies of n-grams of words or POS tags) and content-related (words from grammatical, lexical, psychological lexicons, syntactic features etc.) (Koppel, 2006; Fornaciari and Poesio, 2013). For instance, on the example of DECOUR corpus in Italian, the impact of such features on deception detection was investigated: LIWC features (words and sentences statistics, categories frequencies), lemmas n-grams frequencies and POS tags n-grams frequencies (Fornaciari and Poesio, 2013). Experiments for the Dutch language (on the example of CLiPS Stylometry Investigation (CSI) Corpus) detected, by examining the writing style of the author, that texts can be automatically classified as truthful or deceptive. The only features were the token unigrams; F-score and accuracy reached 72.2% (Verhoeven and Daelemans, 2014). In (Rosso and Cagnina, 2017) the impact of psycholinguistic features is also reviewed. So, in (Parapar et al., 2014) it was revealed, based on LIWC word categories, that use of pronouns, emotion words, markers of cognitive complexity, and motion verbs is more implicated in deceptive texts. In (Cano et al., 2014) six types of similar features were investigated while online behaviour studies: bag-of-words (with unigrams, bigrams and trigrams), POS tags as syntactic features, sentiment polarity, content (complexity, readability, length), psycholinguistic features (obtained with LIWC) and discourse patterns (semantic frames of words).

If we study deception detection for different languages, we should also keep in mind possible linguistic and cultural considerations (Rubin 2014). There is a lack of "real" deceptive texts as they are obviously difficult to collect and label, and studies in text-based deception detection have mostly been performed for Romance and Germanic languages (T. Litvinova et al., 2017). There are few studies of deception detection in Slavic languages. In (Litvinova and Litvinova, 2016) the Russian Deception Bank corpus was studied with LIWC 2007 software (with Russian dictionary included). It was found out that average deceptive texts in Russian contain more pronouns (particularly personal ones), more singular and plural first-person pronouns but fewer third-person plural pronouns, fewer adverbs but more negations, numerals, emotional words overall. Deceptive texts have more positive and fewer negative emotion terms, which can be explained by the topic of the texts. Deceptive texts generally contain more words describing cognitive processes and contain considerably fewer words describing perception and particularly Seeing, Feeling but more from the subgroup Hearing. The fact that there is a lot of perception vocabulary in truthful texts compared to deceptive ones accords to the theories of reality monitoring, as was noted in other studies (Newman et al., 2003). There are also fewer punctuation marks in deceptive texts. In the latter research, 104 parameters were taken, a majority of which were LIWC parameters related to POS tags (unigrams), lexical-semantic group, and other frequencies. Frequencies of function words, discourse markers, different pronouns types were also taken into consideration, using special dictionaries. On the basis of the chosen parameters the classifier reached the overall accuracy of 68.3%, so the statistically significant difference between truthful and deceptive texts from the same author, written using an identical theme, was discovered for Russian. The accuracy of the model was also tested individually for males and females. The classification accuracy for males was 73.3 % and 63.3 % for females (O. Litvinova et al., 2017).

In (Pisarevskaya, 2017) the framework of the Rhetorical Structure Theory is used to reveal the differences between structures of truthful and deceptive (fake) news in Russian. The corpus of 134 news reports was collected. The best results for text classification were got by using Support Vector Machines with linear kernel (accuracy 65%). Discourse features (rhetorical relations frequencies and frequencies of their bigrams and trigrams) were taken as features, other possible language features were not taken into consideration.

Therefore, several parameters that are usually used for deception detection are already applied to the Russian language: POS tags and psycholinguistic features from LIWC, discourse features based on the Rhetorical Structure Theory. The impact of other psycholinguistic features, sentiment features, bigrams of POS tags, syntactic features, readability features needs to be studied.

3. Corpus

The only existing freely available corpus of truthful and deceptive texts for the Russian language is the Russian Deception Bank (Litvinova and Litvinova, 2016), so we chose it for our research goals. The corpus consists of 113 text pairs. Each pair contains one truthful and one deceptive narrative written by the same person and on the same topic: "How I spent yesterday". All texts have labels if they are truthful or deceptive. The average length of text is 221 words. The corpus can be downloaded from RusProfiling Lab website (http://en.rusprofilinglab.ru/korpus-tekstov/russian-deception-bank /). There are plans to extend it, but it can be already used for deception detection experiments.

Truthful text	Deceptive text
So here we were in Piter and went to the apartment that we had booked, it was not far from the city centre. Having dropped off our stuff, we went on a walk around the city centre and grabbed something to eat. Well, actually every afternoon we spent here was pretty much the same. In the evening we would go to any Pub or Bar and killed time there. Yes, killed time because it was not much fun. Maybe it's because the people around weren't much fun. Of course it was interesting to visit the museums and other sights of the city but I can't say that really left an impression that it was supposed to and all in all, I didn't feel too happy throughout that trip.	Having come to Piter, first thing we went to the apartment that we had booked, it was in the city centre, straight in Nevskiy, our window overlooked the beautiful views of Piter, especially in the evening when the sun went down, it was very beautiful. Of course you can spend ages walking the streets of the city and never get tired, while you are walking, you can't help being happy about everything you see around you. Every evening we would drive around different places in the city and sure thing, we don't have any clubs or pubs like that back home and I don't think we ever will. The way this city makes you feel is just special.

Table 1: Sample true and deceptive texts from the same author, translated into English (O. Litvinova et al., 2017).

The corpus texts were written by university students, native speakers of Russian. To keep them highly motivated, they were told that their texts would be evaluated by a trained psychologist who would attempt to distinguish a truthful text from a deceptive one, without having preliminary information of which texts are truthful and which are not. The respondents did not know the ultimate aim of the research. Therefore, it let make the texts closer to spontaneously produced written texts and minimize the effect of the observer's paradox.

The corpus was launched in 2014 as part of a text corpus called RusPersonality, Hence, the following metadata, with detailed information about the texts' authors, is provided in the corpus: gender, age, faculty and field of studies, dominant hand, psychological testing results – tests on brain lateral profile, test "Domino", questionnaire "Behaviour Self-Regulation Style". This information can be used in studies into the effects of personality on deception production, because these individual differences could be considered as vital factors in creating an objective method of identifying intentionally deceptive information (Levitan et al., 2015). There are 46 male and 67 female authors in corpus.

4. Features and Research Objectives

Our hypothesis is that there are significant differences between truthful and deceptive texts, and we try to reveal them using different types of markers and compare the results. The corpus also enables personal features of authors (psychological and physical), and we can check if they can be considered as a factor contributing to the production of their deceptive texts.

The corpus was already processed using LIWC software that is used in most studies of text-based deception detection (O. Litvinova et al., 2017), so psycholinguistic specialties from LIWC are already investigated and we do not take them into consideration now. However, we take POS tags frequencies, although they were already investigated, and analyze them together with POS tags bigrams frequencies.

There are three groups of markers for each text.

The first group is built by psycholinguistic and sentiment markers. We use four psycholinguistic properties of words from the MRC Psycholinguistic Database: familiarity, concreteness, imagery, average age of acquisition. Familiarity can be undestood as the frequency with which a word is seen, heard or used daily. Age of acquisition means the age at which a word is believed to be learned. Level of concreteness means how tangible the described object is. Imagery means the intensity with which a word arouses images (Paetzold and Specia, 2016). We use the bootstrapped version of these properties presented in (Paetzold and Specia, 2016), it contains information about 85942 words. We take the normalized frequencies in texts as features. As there are no such databases for Russian, we suggested that these properties could be universal for different languages and, hence, translated the corpus texts into English for the study of this group of markers. We use the API of Yandex machine translation service (http://translate.yandex.ru/) for translation from Russian into English.

Sentiment features are normalized frequencies of positive and negative sentiment words, taken separately or together as common sentiment words, so we have three features for them. We use lemmas from the General Russian Sentiment Lexicon (RuSentiLex) (Loukachevitch and Levchik, 2016) (http://www.labinform.ru/pub/rusentilex/rusentilex_2017.txt). It contains more than 12000 sentiment words and phrases, with positive, negative, neutral, positive/negative sentiment orientation. We take only positive and negative words from the lexicon.

We also add, as separate features, normalized frequencies of words that reflect 36 different emotions and attitudes: Worry, Friendship, Regret, Sadness, Sincerity, Double-Dealing, Curiosity, Love, Hope, Impertinence, Dissatisfaction, Disfavour, Disbelief, Grievance, Loneliness, Acceptance, Protest, Joy, Disinterest, Courage, Humility, Doubt, Calmness, Fear, Shame, Surprise, Pleasure, Respect, Inspiration, Belief, Call, Selfassumption, Pity, Desire, Cruelty, Anger.

The second group includes normalized frequencies of 11 POS tags and POS tags bigrams. First-person personal pronouns are considered separately. There are 204 possible bigrams collocations in corpus. Punctuation marks and whitespaces are not excluded from the analysis for bigrams and get their own tags.

The third group is presented by syntactic and readability features. We use two readability features: the Automated Readability Index and the Coleman–Liau Readability Formula. Here we also consider average length of tokens for text, type-token ratio, normalized frequencies of exclamation marks, question marks, and two types of Russian participles (the first type is 'prichastie' and the second type is 'deeprichastie'). Syntactic features consist of 18 parameters that reflect structures of compound sentences and parenthetical constructions. These parameters names are in Russian and are taken from the Russian National Corpus (http://www.ruscorpora.ru).

5. Experiments and Data Analysis

Main experiments. For the whole data set, for each group of markers we run two experiments: with Support Vector Machines (linear kernel) (SVM) classifier and with Random Forest classifier. So we can reveal differences between truthful and deceptive texts, compare the impact of three groups of markers on the deception detection and find out, for each group, which subgroup is more important (Tables 2-4).

As **additional experiments**, we take texts of two groups of respondents (female and male authors separately), as in the previous work based on this corpus (Litvinova et al., 2017), to find out if there are any gender specified differences between truthful and deceptive texts. The experiments are run on the example of Random Forest classifier (Table 5).

The baseline for all experiments is 50%, because there is the equal number of truthful and deceptive narratives in the corpus.

We also try to reveal statistically significant parameters for truthful/deceptive texts for the whole data set and for the texts of female/male authors, taken separately (Table 6), using Student's t-test p-value.

Results for psycholinguistic and sentiment markers can be estimated to be the same as chance results (Table 2). These markers also do not show many statistically significant differences between truthful and deceptive texts. For the whole data set, the only statistically significant feature is Pleasure attitude.

The impact of syntactic and readabililty markers, taken together or separately, on the binary classification task is also not high (Table 3). Most of them do not reveal any statistically significant differences between truthful and deceptive narratives for the whole data set (p-value is <=0.05 for only one feature — 'разъяснительное' syntactical relation). Meanwhile, syntactic features are more important for classification than readability features, and the most important parameters are 'подчинительно-союзное' and 'релятивное' syntactical relations.

POS tags markers and POS tags bigrams markers can help more to detect truthful and deceptive texts, it corresponds to the results in (O. Litvinova, 2017). Accuracy for SVM classification is 0.57. The impact of POS tags features is more important than the impact of POS tags bigrams (Table 4). Conjunctions, interjections and numerals are mostly important for classification. Several features reveal statistically significant differences between truthful and deceptive texts for the whole data set (Table 6).

Texts by female/male authors, analyzed separately, help to reveal more statistically significant parameters for detection if a text is truthful or deceptive (Table 6).

In Table 5, we can see that the results for texts of female and male authors taken separately. Here we can also estimate that classification for the whole data set, based on POS tags markers and POS tags bigram markers, is the best one.

We can conclude that POS tags and POS tags bigrams features are mostly important for the automated deception detection for the Russian language.

	Random Forest Classifier, 5-fold cross-validation			
	Precision	Recall	F-measure	Accuracy
Sentiment features	0.29	0.6	0.39	0.48
Emotion features	0.48	0.45	0.46	0.48
Psycholinguistic features	0.45	0.44	0.44	0.45
Sentiment+ emotion+ psycholinguistic features	0.49	0.44	0.46	0.49
	Support Vector Machines (linear kernel), 5-fold cross-validation			
Sentiment features	0.19	0.4	0.25	0.48
Emotion features	0.47	0.46	0.46	0.47
Psycholinguistic features	0.42	0.46	0.42	0.42
Sentiment+ emotion+ psycholinguistic features	0.47	0.54	0.49	0.46

Table 2: Results for psycholinguistic and sentiment features (the whole data set).

	Random Forest Classifier, 5-fold cross-validation			
	Precision	Recall	F-measure	Accuracy
Syntactic features	0.52	0.49	0.49	0.50
Readablilty features	0.46	0.46	0.45	0.45
Syntactic+ readability features	0.49	0.46	0.46	0.48
	Support Vector Machines (linear kernel), 5-fold cross-validation			
Syntactic features	0.56	0.53	0.54	0.55
Readability features	0.55	0.30	0.26	0.45
Syntactic+ readability features	0.51	0.50	0.50	0.50

Table 3: Results for syntactic features and readability features (the whole data set).

	Random Forest Classifier, 5-fold cross-validation			
	Precision	Recall	F-measure	Accuracy
POS tags features	0.43	0.46	0.44	0.43
POS tags bigrams features	0.51	0.49	0.49	0.50
POS tags+ POS tags bigrams features	0.40	0.39	0.39	0.42
	Support Vector Machines (linear kernel), 5-fold cross-validation			
POS tags features	0.54	0.63	0.57	0.54
POS tags bigrams features	0.50	0.49	0.48	0.48
POS tags+ POS tags bigrams features	0.59	0.56	0.56	0.57

Table 4: Results for POS tags features and POS tags bigrams features (the whole data set).

	Random Forest Classifier, 5-fold cross-validation			
	Precision	Recall	F-measure	Accuracy
Psycholinguistic and sentiment features (the first group)				
The whole data set	0.49	0.44	0.46	0.49
Female authors	0.44	0.48	0.45	0.45
Male authors	0.47	0.53	0.49	0.46
POS tags and POS tags bigrams (the second group)				
The whole data set	0.52	0.45	0.46	0.51
Female authors	0.43	0.50	0.43	0.40
Male authors	0.51	0.46	0.46	0.48
Syntactic and readability features (the third group)				
The whole data set	0.49	0.46	0.46	0.48
Female authors	0.56	0.46	0.48	0.52
Male authors	0.47	0.40	0.42	0.46
The first group+the second group+the third group				
The whole data set	0.45	0.45	0.45	0.45

Table 5: Classification results for texts of female and male authors.

6. Conclusions and Discussion

We studied the impact of basic lexical and syntactic factors, which were not studied and compared before for the Russian language deception detection methods, on the successful deception detection. We revealed that POS tags and POS tags bigrams features are mostly important for binary classification task (the accuracy with SVM is 0.57), and conjunctions, interjections and numerals are the most significant parameters. Syntactic features should be also taken into consideration in further research. The results are preliminary and should be double-checked later on bigger Russian corpora. Other classification methods should be also tried to get better accuracy. The topic should be studied more deeply and intensively, on higher levels of linguistic processing, using semantics, discourse and pragmatics features. It could help search engines to label retrieved documents as reliable or not.

Group of markers	Texts by female authors: statistically significant parameters for truthful/ deceptive texts	Texts by male authors: statistically significant parameters for truthful/ deceptive texts	Texts from the whole dataset: statistically significant parameters for truthful/ deceptive texts
Psycholinguistic and sentiment features	Pleasure, Fear	Curiosity, Loneliness, Inspiration	Pleasure
POS tags and POS tags bigrams (here: excluding whitespaces and punctuation marks)	collocations: adverb-like pronoun+ adjective, numeral+ adjective-like pronoun, particle+ adverb	collocations: conjunction+ conjunction; conjunction+ adjective-like pronoun	numerals, collocations: conjunction+ conjunction, conjunction+adjective, noun-like pronoun+ conjunction, particle+ adverb, conjunction+adjective
Syntactic and readability features	'разъяснительное', 'сравнительное', 'сравнительно-союзное' syntactical relations	-	'разъяснительное' syntactical relation

Table 6: Differences for texts written by male authors and texts written by female authors: p-value is <=0.05.

Acknowledgments

This research is supported by a grant from the Russian Foundation for Basic Research, N 15-34-01221 Lie Detection in a Written Text: A Corpus Study.

References

G.D. Bond and A.Y. Lee. 2005. Language of lies in prison: Linguistic classification of prisoners' truthful and deceptive natural language. Applied Cognitive Psychology, 19(3), pages 313-329.

A.E. Cano, M. Fernandez, and H. Alani. 2014. Detecting Child Grooming Behaviour Patterns on Social Media. Social informatics, ed. L. Aiello and D. McFarland, Lecture notes in computer science, vol. 8851, Springer. pages 412-427.

C. Chen, H. Zhao, and Y. Yang. 2015. Deceptive Opinion Spam Detection Using Deep Level Linguistic Features. In NLPCC 2015, LNAI 9362, pages 465–474.

R. Clark. 2014. Top 8 Secrets of How to Write an Upworthy Headline, Poynter, URL: http://www.poynter.org/news/media-innovation/255886/top-8-secrets-of-how-to-write-an-upworthy-headline/

B.M. DePaulo, K. Charlton, H. Cooper, J.J. Lindsay, and L. Muhlenbruck. 1997. The Accuracy-Confidence Correlation in the Detection of Deception. Personality & Social Psychology Review, 1(4), pages 346-357.

B.M. DePaulo, J.J. Lindsay, B.E. Malone, L. Muhlenbruck, K. Charlton, and H. Cooper. 2003. Cues to deception. Psychological bulletin, 129(1), pages 74-118.

R.K. Dewang and A.K. Singh. 2017. Spam Review Detection through Lexical Chain Based Semantic Similarity Algorithm (LCBSS) for Negative Reviews. International Journal of Engineering and Technology (IJET). 8(6), Dec 2016-Jan 2017, pages 2946-2955.

S. Feng, R. Banerjee, and Y. Choi. 2012. Syntactic stylometry for deception detection. In Proceedings of the 50th Annual Meeting of the Association for Computational Linguistics (Volume 2: Short Papers), Jeju Island, Korea, July, pages 171–175.

V. Feng and G. Hirst. 2013. Detecting deceptive opinion with profile compatibility. In Proceedings of the 6th International Joint Conference on Natural Language Processing. Nagoya, Yapan, pages 14-18.

T. Fornaciari and M. Poesio. 2013. Automatic deception detection in Italian court cases. Artificial Intelligence and Law, 21(3), pages 303-340.

Ch.M. Fuller, D.P. Biros, and D. Dursun. 2008. Exploration of Feature Selection and Advanced Classification Models for High-Stakes Deception Detection. In Proceedings of the 41st Annual Hawaii International Conference on System Sciences, IEEE. Waikoloa, HI, USA.

C.M. Fuller, D.P Biros, and R.L. Wilson. 2009. Decision support for determining veracity via linguistic-based cues. Decision Support Systems, 46(3), pages 695-703.

J.T. Hancock, C. Toma, and N. Ellison. 2007a. The truth about lying in online dating profiles. In Proceedings of the SIGCHI conference on Human factors in computing systems. ACM, pages 449-452.

J.T. Hancock, L.E. Curry, S. Goorha, and M. Woodworth. 2007b. On lying and being lied to: A linguistic analysis of deception in computer-mediated communication. Discourse Processes, 45(1), pages 1-23.

J. Hancock, M. Woodworth, and S. Porter. 2011. Hungry like a wolf: A word pattern analysis of the language of psychopaths. Legal and Criminological Psychology, 18, pages 102-114.

M. Hardalov, I. Koychev, and P. Nakov. 2016. In Search of Credible News. In Artificial Intelligence: Methodology, Systems, and Applications, pages 172-180.

A. Heidari, M. D'Arienzo, S.A. Crossley, and N. Duran. 2017. Computational Analysis of Lexical and Cohesion Differences in Deceptive Language: The Role of Accordance. In Proceedings of 30th International Florida Artificial Intelligence Research Society Conference. May 2017, pages 270-275.

J. Hirschberg, S. Benus, J. Brenier, F. Enos, S. Friedman, S. Gilman, C. Gir, G. Graciarena, A. Kathol, and L. Michaelis. 2005. Distinguishing deceptive from non-deceptive speech. In Proceedings of Interspeech 2005, Lisbon, Portugal, ACM, pages 1833–1836.

M. Koppel, J. Schler, S. Argamon, and J. Pennebaker. 2006. Effects of age and gender on blogging. In Computational Approaches to Analyzing Weblogs, Papers from the 2006 AAAI Spring Symposium, Technical Report SS-06-03, Stanford, California, USA, March 27-29.

N. Kumar and R.N. Reddy. 2012. Automatic Detection of Fake Profiles in Online Social Networks. BTech Thesis.

D.J. Lary, A. Nikitkov, and D. Stone. 2010. Which Machine-Learning Models Best Predict Online Auction Seller Deception Risk? American Accounting Association AAA Strategic and Emerging Technologies.

S.I. Levitan, M. Levine, J. Hirschberg, N. Cestero, G. An, and A. Rosenberg. 2015. Individual Differences in Deception and Deception Detection. In COGNITIVE 2015: The Seventh International Conference on Advanced Cognitive Technologies and Application.

E. Lex, A. Juffinger, and M. Granitzer. 2010. Objectivity classification in online media. In Proceedings of the 21st ACM conference on Hypertext and hypermedia, pages 293-294.

J. Li, M. Ott, and C. Cardie. 2013. Identifying Manipulated Offerings on Review Portals. In Proceedings of the 2013 Conference on Empirical Methods in Natural Language Processing, Seattle, Washington, USA, 18-21 October 2013, pages 1933-1942.

O. Litvinova, T. Litvinova, P. Seredin, and J. Lyell. 2017. Deception Detection in Russian Texts. In Proceedings of the Student Research Workshop at the 15th Conference of the European Chapter of the Association for Computational Linguistics, Valencia, Spain, April 3-7, pages 43–52.

T. Litvinova and O. Litvinova. 2016. Russian Deception Bank: A Corpus for Automated Deception Detection in Text. In Proceedings of CBBLR 2016, Tribun EU, pages 1-7.

T. Litvinova, E. Ryzhkova, O. Litvinova, E. Larin, J. Lyell, and P. Seredin. 2017. Building a corpus of real texts for deception detection. In IMS'17, June 21–23, 2017, St. Petersburg, Russia.

N. Loukachevitch and A. Levchik. 2016. Creating a General Russian Sentiment Lexicon. In Proceedings of Language Resources and Evaluation Conference LREC-2016.

R. Mihalcea and C. Strapparava. 2009. The Lie Detector: Explorations in the Automatic Recognition of Deceptive Language. In Proceedings of the Association for Computational Linguistics (ACL-IJCNLP 2009), ACM, pages 309-312.

S. Mukherjee, S. Dutta, and G. Weikum. 2016. Credible Review Detection with Limited Information using Consistency Features. Machine Learning and Knowledge Discovery in Databases, pages 195-213.

M. Newman, J. Pennebaker, D. Berry, and J. Richards. 2003. Lying words: Predicting deception from linguistic style. Personality and Social Psychology Bulletin, 29, pages 665-675.

M. Ott, Y. Choi, C. Cardie, and J.T. Hancock. 2011. Finding deceptive opinion spam by any stretch of the imagination. In Proceedings of the 49th Annual Meeting of the Association for Computational Linguistics: Human Language Technologies, Portland, Oregon, USA, June, pages 309–319.

M. Ott, C. Cardie, and J. Hancock. 2013. Negative Deceptive Opinion Spam. In Proceedings of NAACLHLT, pages 497–501.

G.H. Paetzold and L. Specia. 2016. Inferring Psycholinguistic Properties of Words. In Proceedings of NAACL-HLT 2016, San Diego, California, June 12-17, pages 435–440.

J. Parapar, D.E. Losada, and Á. Barreiro. 2014. Combining Psycho-linguistic, Content-based and Chat-based Features to Detect Predation in Chatrooms. Journal of Universal Computer Science, 20(2), pages 213-239.

J. Pennebaker and M. Francis. 1999. Linguistic inquiry & word count: LIWC. Erlbaum Publishers.

D. Pisarevskaya. 2017. Rhetorical Structure Theory as a Feature for Deception Detection in News Reports in the Russian Language. In Computationa Linguistics and Intellectual Technologies. Papers from the Annual International Conference 'Dialogue' (2017). Moscow, May 31-June 3, 16(1), pages 191-200.

S. Porter and J.C. Yuille. 1996. The language of deceit: An investigation of the verbal clues to deception in the interrogation context. Law & Human Behavior, 20 (4), pages 443-458.

P. Rosso and L.C. Cagnina. 2017. Deception Detection and Opinion Spam. Chapter in Book A Practical Guide to Sentiment Analysis, ed. E. Cambria et al. Springer International Publishing AG 2017, pages 155-171.

V.L. Rubin. 2014. Pragmatic and Cultural Considerations for Deception Detection in Asian Languages. In ACM Transactions on Asian Language Information Processing, Vol. 13, No. 2, Article 10, Publication date: June 2014, pages 10:1-10:8.

R. Sauri and J. Pustejovsky. 2012. Are You Sure That This Happened? Assessing the Factuality Degree of Events in Text. Computational Linguistics, 38(2), pages 261-299.

C. Strapparava and A. Valitutti. 2004. WordNet-Affect: an Affective Extension of WordNet. In Proceedings of the 4th International Conference on Language Resources and Evaluation (LREC 2004), Lisbon, May 2004, pages 1083-1086.

C.L.Toma and J.T. Hancock. 2012. What Lies Beneath: The Linguistic Traces of Deception in Online Dating Profiles. Journal of Communication, 62(1), pages 78-97.

B. Verhoeven and W. Daelemans. 2014. CLIPS Stylometry Investigation (CSI) Corpus: a Dutch Corpus for the Detection of Age, Gender, Personality, Sentiment and Deception in Text. In: Proceedings of the Ninth International Conference on Language Resources and Evaluation (LREC'14), isbn 978-2-9517408-8-4, ELRA: Reykjavik, Iceland, pages 3081-3085.

H. Zhang, S. Wei, H. Tan, and J. Zheng. 2009. Deception detection based on SVM for Chinese text in CMC. In Proceedings of Sixth International Conference on Information Technology: New Generations (ITNG '09) (Las Vegas, NV, USA, April 27-29, 2009), IEEE, pages 481–486.

L. Zhou, J. Burgoon, J. Nunamaker, and D. Twitchell. 2004. Automating linguistics-based cues for detecting deception in text-based asynchronous computer-mediated communications. Group Decision & Negotiation, 13(1), pages 81-106.

oIQa: An Opinion Influence Oriented Question Answering Framework with Applications to Marketing Domain

Dumitru-Clementin Cercel, Cristian Onose, Stefan Trausan-Matu and **Florin Pop**
Faculty of Automatic Control and Computers
University Politehnica of Bucharest, Romania
clementin.cercel@gmail.com, onose.cristian@gmail.com,
stefan.trausan@cs.pub.ro, florin.pop@cs.pub.ro

Abstract

Understanding questions and answers in Question Answering (QA) system is a major challenge in the domain of natural language processing. In this paper, we present a question answering system that influences the human opinions in a conversation. The opinion words are quantified by using a lexicon-based method. We apply Latent Semantic Analysis and the cosine similarity measure between candidate answers and each question to infer the answer of the bot.

1 Introduction

In the past decade, electronic commerce has seen a strong and steady growth causing more and more companies to invest in it. Also, large numbers of users express their opinions about many topics in social media, which has become a means of influencing users to make certain decisions. As such, product or services reviews have become an important part of the purchase journey for customers.

More and more users recognize that reviews influence their buying decision to the point that some consider them to carry as much trust as recommendations from their friends or family.

In this paper, we integrate the influence concept in a traditional question answering system. The hypothesis that underlies our research is that human opinions may change over time as a consequence of the interaction with a chatbot in a question-answering system. A human participating in a question-answering system is influenced over time by the chatbot if he shares beliefs with it for a given amount of the conversation. Thus, influence is analyzed by taking into consideration the changes in human opinions.

The posts in our question-answering system are preprocessed by means of a Natural Language Processing (NLP) tool (De Marneffe et al., 2006) to identify the dependency relations between words. Using dependency relations specific for opinion mining, we extract opinion words.

Opinion lexicons represent important resources for identifying the sentiment of opinion words. In this paper, we adopt an opinion lexicon-based method to identify the sentiment expressed by each opinion word. There are available several opinion lexicons that enable us to classify opinion words into one of the following sentiment categories: positive, negative, or neutral. In this way, we classify the opinion words by using the following four opinions lexicons (Cercel and Trausan-Matu, 2014a): SentiWordNet (Baccianella and Sebastiani, 2010), Micro-WNOp (Cerini et al., 2007), MPQA subjectivity lexicon (Wilson et al., 2005), and Bing Liu's opinion lexicon (Hu and Liu, 2004).

Using several opinion lexicons is necessary mainly due to the fact that there is no single opinion lexicon that returns the exact sentiment given both the context and the domain in which the opinion words are referenced.

We proposed a model for question-level sentiment analysis, where many opinions that have different sentiments are expressed. In this model, we take into consideration the sentiment strength expressed by opinions.

Finally, we apply Latent Semantic Analysis (Landauer et al., 1998) and the cosine similarity measure between candidate answers and each question to infer the answer of the bot.

This paper is structured as follows. In Section 2, we briefly discuss the existing approaches to the

Proceedings of Natural Language Processing and Information Retrieval Workshop, pages 11–18,
Varna, Bulgaria, Sep 7 2017.

question answering task. In Section 3, we detail the system proposed by us to solve the problem of opinion influence oriented question answering. The experimental results are shown in Section 4. Finally, Section 5 is dedicated to the conclusions of our research.

2 Related Work

The work presented in this paper is best described as the combination of social influence and two broad NLP areas of interest: opinion mining (also known as sentiment analysis) and question-answering systems. The problem of review corpus based question-answering systems has seen some interest in the past (McAuley and Yang, 2016; Wan and McAuley, 2016), and also opinion mining techniques have been incorporated into such setups to provide more personalized answers to subjective queries (Wan and McAuley, 2016; Balahur et al., 2009a). However, to our knowledge, a question-answering system with the ability to influence the opinion of users is a novel idea.

QA systems. Their aim is to automatically provide answers to questions submitted by users in natural language. Given different attributes these systems can be classified in a number of categories (Mishra and Jain, 2016). Our main interest is regarding how the input of the user is handled: (1) Corpus based QAs select candidate answers from a dataset based on different similarity measures; (2) QAs that extract concepts and relations between them from the inputs and formulate an answer.

We focused on corpus based types (i.e. user reviews) because these kinds of datasets are commonly available. An important aspect for this type of QAs is the task of identifying quality candidate answers for a given user query (Anderson et al., 2012; Yuen et al., 2011).

Opinion mining is a research field of great interest because many applications are based on opinion mining, including opinion summarization (Balahur et al., 2009b), opinion propagation (Cercel and Trausan-Matu, 2014b) and sentiment prediction (Kim et al., 2013). We classify the types of granularity studied in sentiment analysis as: the document-level sentiment classification, the sentence-level sentiment classification, and the word-level sentiment classification. Methods of identifying the sentiment expressed by an opinion word can be classified into: manual methods, corpus-based methods, and opinion lexicon-based methods (Liu, 2012).

Social Influence. In social influence analysis, several methods have been proposed to measure the influence among users. For example, Tang et al. (2009) studied influence probabilities on different topics in a social network. Also, Liu et al. (2010) studied the modeling of indirect influence in heterogeneous networks, focusing on users' behaviors such as following, citing, and replying. Apart from the methods presented above, different types of social influence are described in social influence analysis. For instance, conformity is a form of social influence in which people change their opinions or behavior in order to be assimilated into a group (Tang et al., 2013).

3 Approach

The proposed method consists of several modules described below.

3.1 Sentiment Analysis

3.1.1 Opinion Extraction from Questions

The goal of this step is to identify opinion words in a given question. We consider that the target entity to which the opinions refers is syntactically defined by a noun term, also opinion words can be one of the following parts of speech: adjective, adverb, or verb.

The questions are preprocessed by means of the Stanford CoreNLP tool (De Marneffe and Manning, 2008) to identify the dependency relations between words. Each dependency relation is a binary grammatical relation between a *governor* word (also called *head*) and a *dependent* word. A dependency relation is represented in the form: *abbreviated relation name (governor, dependent)*, where the dependency relation exists between the *governor* word and the *dependent* word.

Using specific rules for opinion mining, we extract dependency relations which identify opinion words. There rules are given in the form of syntactic dependency relation between a noun term and the opinion word. In Table 1, we have summarized the dependency relations from Stanford CoreNLP used to extract opinion words.

The algorithm for dependency relations extraction (see Algorithm 1) receives as input the entire question and outputs relations in the form of *(noun term, opinion word)* pairs.

Dependency Relations	Description
dobj (“direct object”)	The opinion word is a verb or a complement following a copular verb
nsubj (“nominal subject”)	The opinion word is a complement following a copular verb
amod (“adjectival modifier”)	The opinion word is the adjectival modifier of a noun
advmod (“adverbial modifier”)	The opinion word is an adverbial modifier of a verb
acomp (“adjectival complement”)	The opinion word is the adverbial complement of a verb
xcomp (“open clausal complement”)	The opinion word is the complement following a copular verb
neg (“negation modifier”)	The opinion word sentiment is shifted by negation word

Table 1: The list of dependency relations used for opinion extraction.

We start by running the question through Stanford CoreNLP which determines all dependency relations (A1 : 2). For each dependency relation we identify if it is fitting for discovering opinion words by analyzing the rules in Table 1 (A1 : 3-23).

Algorithm 1: Identifying Stanford Dependency Relations for Opinion Mining

```
Input: q – question
Output: Ω – a set of pairs (noun term, opinion word)
 1: Ω ← Ø
 2: R ← Parse(q) // the set {rel_j(h_k, d_l)}_{j,k,l∈N} of
        all dependency relations between the words
 3: for each dependency relation rel_j(h_k, d_l) in R do
 4:   if rel_j = "dobj" and checkVerb(h_k) and checkNoun(d_l) then
 5:       Ω ← Ω ∪ (h_k, d_l)
 6:   end if
 7:   if rel_j = "nsubj" and checkAdjective(h_k) and checkNoun(d_l) then
 8:       Ω ← Ω ∪ (h_k, d_l)
 9:   end if
10:     if rel_j ="amod" and checkAdjective(h_l) and checkNoun(d_k) then
11:         Ω ← Ω ∪ (d_l, h_k)
12:     end if
13:     if rel_j = "advmod" and checkVerb(d_l) and there is rel_jj(h_kk, d_ll) so that
14:         rel_jj = "rcmod" and d_k = h_kk then
15:         Ω ← Ω ∪ (h_l, d_ll)
16:     end if
17:     if rel_j = "acomp" and checkVerb(h_k) and there is rel_jj(h_kk, d_ll) so that rel_jj = "rcmod" and h_k = d_ll then
18:         Ω ← Ω ∪ (d_l, h_kk)
19:     end if
20:     if rel_j = "xcomp" and checkVerb(h_i,k) and there is rel_jj(h_kk, d_ll) so that rel_jj = "ccomp" and h_k = d_ll then
21:         Ω ← Ω ∪ (h_kk, d_l)
22:     end if
23:   end for
```

For usability purposes, the opinions are modeled by numerical values. To accomplish this, the opinion words, that are extracted from questions, are encoded as follows: -1, 0, or +1, where a value of -1 corresponds to an opinion word with negative sentiment, a value of 0 corresponds to an opinion word with neutral sentiment, and a value of +1 corresponds to an opinion word with positive sentiment.

3.1.2 Opinion Word-Level Sentiment Identification

After the step of extracting opinion words from questions, we proceed to determine the sentiment expressed by each opinion word. For the task of identifying the sentiment of opinion words, we have decided upon four opinion lexicons that we have used in our experiments as follows:

- SentiWordNet (Baccianella and Sebastiani, 2010) is an opinion lexicon in which the synsets, which are part of the WordNet lexical database (Fellbaum, 1998), are defined by three sentiment scores: positive score, negative score and neutral score. Each sentiment score is a numerical value from the interval [0, 1] so that the sum of the three sentiment scores for each synset is 1. SentiWordNet contains over 155,000 words from 117,659 synsets.

- Micro-WNOp (Cerini et al., 2007) is composed of a subset of WordNet synsets more precisely 1,105 synsets, which represent 1,960 distinct words. Every Micro-WNOp synset is annotated with two numerical scores: one score indicates the grade of positivity of its component words, and the other one indicates the grade of negativity. Both scores have values between 0 and 1, and their sum is less than or equal to 1.

- MPQA Subjectivity Lexicon (Wilson et al., 2005) as single-word clues. The sentiment expressed by each clue was manually annotated in one of the following categories: positive, negative, both (positive and negative), or neutral.

- Bing Liu Lexicon (Hu and Liu, 2004) is a list of 6,785 words divided into two sets according to their sentiment: a set of words with positive sentiment and another set of words with negative sentiment.

Since the lexicons have various ways of representing the sentiment score, it becomes necessary to use specific algorithms for each opinion lexicon in order to map the output to numerical values, as outlined below.

SentiWordNet: The outline of the algorithm based on SentiWordNet for determining the sentiment of an input opinion word is shown in Algorithm 1. Initially, the algorithm establishes if the input opinion word, that corresponds to a given part of speech, is not part of SentiWordNet. If this is the case then it will return the sentiment score of 0 (A2 : 1-3), otherwise all the sense numbers of the input word will be arranged in ascending order (A2 : 4). For each of the sorted senses we compute the difference between the positive score and the negative score returned by SentiWordNet (A2 : 6). If the difference is zero, and the positive score is non-zero, the algorithm continues with the next iteration (A2 : 7-9). If the difference is zero, and the positive score is also zero, then the output sentiment is neutral (A2 : 10-12). If the difference is greater than zero, then the sentiment is positive (A2 : 13-15). If the difference is less than zero, then the sentiment is negative (A2 : 16-18). Finally, if the input opinion word has the positive score equal to the negative score for all its senses, then the sentiment is considered positive (A2 : 20).

Algorithm 2 (A2): Opinion Word Sentiment Identification using SentiWordNet

Input: w – opinion word;
Input: pos – part of speech for the opinion word *w*;
Output: a value ∈ {-1, 0, +1} – indicates the sentiment of the opinion word *w*, where: -1 denotes a negative sentiment, 0 denotes a neutral sentiment, and +1 denotes a positive sentiment;

```
1: if !FindOpinionWord(w, pos) then
2:    return 0
3: end if
4: S ← GetSenses(w, pos)
5: for each s ∈ S do
6: diff ← GetPositiveScore(w, s) - GetNegativeScore(w, s)
7: if diff = 0 and GetPositiveScore(w, s) != 0 then
8:    continue
9: end if
10: if diff = 0 and GetPositiveScore(w, s) = 0 then
11:    return 0
12: end if
13: if diff > 0 then
14:    return +1
15: end if
16: if diff < 0 then
17:    return -1
18: end if
19: end for
20: return +1
```

Micro-WNOp: Micro-WNOp is a human annotated lexicon that can be broken into three parts. In the initial stage five human evaluators work together, while for the other parts they are split into groups that work independently from one another. Each opinion word is given a positive sentiment score and a negative sentiment score regardless of the way the groups are formed. Because the groups work separately, there are differences between the scores. To solve this issue, we consider that the sentiment of an opinion word is given by the first evaluator's annotation. The algorithm based on Micro-WNOp resembles the algorithm that uses SentiWordNet which is shown in Algorithm 2.

Bing Liu Lexicon: The summary of the algorithm based on Bing Liu's opinion lexicon for determining the sentiment of an input opinion word is shown in Algorithm 3. For the Bing Liu's opinion lexicon, we assign a sentiment score of +1 to each opinion word in the positive list (A3 : 4-6), and a sentiment score of -1 to each opinion word in the negative list (A3 : 7-9). Also, if the opinion word is not found in the lexicon the algorithm outputs a sentiment score of 0 (A3 : 1-2).

Algorithm 3 (A3): Opinion Word Sentiment Identification using Bing Liu's opinion lexicon

Input: w – opinion word;
Output a value ∈ {-1, +1} – indicates the sentiment of the opinion word *w*, where: -1 denotes a negative sentiment and +1 denotes a positive sentiment;

```
1: if !FindOpinionWord(w) then
2:    return 0
3: else
```

```
if w ∈ GetPositiveList() then
    return +1
end if
if w ∈ GetNegativeList() then
    return -1
end if
end if
```

MPQA Subjectivity Lexicon: The algorithm, that uses the MPQA subjectivity lexicon, for determining the sentiment of an input opinion word is described in Algorithm 4. For the MPQA subjectivity lexicon, the algorithm associates the sentiment scores of -1, 0, or +1 to the lexicons' outputted categorical values of negative, neutral or positive, respectively (A4 : 5-16). What's more in this lexicon, opinion words can be annotated with both positive and negative classes. In this case, we assign the sentiment score of +1 to the opinion words. Finally, if the input word is not found in the lexicon, then the returned sentiment score is 0 (A4 : 1-2).

Algorithm 4 (A4): Opinion Word Sentiment Identification using the MPQA subjectivity lexicon

Input: w – opinion word;
Input: pos – part of speech for the opinion word *w*;
Output: a value ∈ {-1, 0, +1} – indicates the sentiment of the opinion word *w*, where: -1 denotes a negative sentiment, 0 denotes a neutral sentiment, and +1 denotes a positive sentiment;

```
1: if !FindOpinionWord(w, pos) then
2:     return 0
3: else
4:     polarity ← GetPolarity(w)
5:     if polarity = "positive" then
6:         return +1
7:     end if
8:     if polarity = "negative" then
9:         return -1
10:    end if
11:    if polarity = "neutral" then
12:        return 0
13:    end if
14:    if polarity = "both" then
15:        return +1
16:    end if
17: end if
```

3.1.3 Question-Level Sentiment Identification

Question-level sentiment identification determines whether a subjective question expresses a positive, negative, or neutral sentiment. We determine the sentiment of a question by taking into account the sentiment strength of its opinion words. Let q be a question in the conversation. The sentiment score for the question q is given by the following equation:

$$score(q) = \frac{\sum_{i=1 \wedge w \in S_J^i \wedge w \in S_R^i}^{4} score(w) * \lambda_i}{\sum_{i=1}^{4} |S_J^i| + \sum_{i=1}^{4} |S_R^i| + |S_V|} + \frac{\sum_{w \in S_V} score(w) * \lambda_4}{\sum_{i=1}^{4} |S_J^i| + \sum_{i=1}^{4} |S_R^i| + |S_V|}$$

where:
score(w) = the sentiment score of the opinion word *w* and is calculated by using the opinion lexicons as described above;
S^1_J = the list of adjectives in the superlative;
S^2_J = the list of adjectives in the comparative of superiority;
S^3_J = the list of adjectives in the comparative of inferiority;
S^4_J = the list of adjectives in other degree;
S^1_R = the list of adverbs in the superlative;
S^2_R = the list of adverbs in the comparative of superiority;
S^3_R = the list of adverbs in the comparative of inferiority;
S^4_R = the list of adverbs in other degree;
S_V = the list of verbs;
and | • | denotes the size of list.
The variables λ_1, λ_2, λ_3, and λ_4 take the values 0.9, 0.6, -0.6, and 0.3, respectively. The question q is considered to express a positive sentiment if $score(q) \in (0, +1]$, a negative sentiment if $score(q) \in [-1, 0)$, and a positive sentiment if $score(q) = 0$.

3.2 Answer Selection

The process of answer generation sums up to choosing the answer that is the closest to the question from a semantic point of view. Besides semantic similarity, we also impose the constraint that the answer-level sentiment score has to be positive or neutral. We accomplish this by using Latent Semantic Analysis (LSA) and the cosine similarity measure between candidate answers and each question. Candidate answers are selected from the Stanford Sentiment Treebank dataset (Socher et al., 2013).

3.2.1 Latent Semantic Analysis

LSA is a method used in natural language processing to measure the semantic similarity between two texts. The idea behind this method is that similar texts comprise words with the same or approximately the same meaning.

LSA is a corpus based method that requires a series of document $D = \{d_1, d_2, ..., d_n\}$ for the training step. Let $W = \{w_1, w_2, ..., w_m\}$ be a set consisting of all the distinct terms in the corpus D. Let the number of documents in the corpus be D and the number of terms in the set W be n and m, respectively. The LSA method starts by creating a term-document matrix $A = \{a_{i,j}\}$ of dimension $m \times n$, where the column j^{th} in the matrix A corresponds to the document d_j in the corpus D, and the row i^{th} in the matrix A corresponds to the term w_i in the set W. The entry $a_{i,j}$ in the term-document matrix represents the total number of occurrences of the term $w_i \in W$ in the document $d_j \in D$.

Using the operation called Singular Value Decomposition (SVD), taken from linear algebra, the matrix A is decomposed into three matrices U, Σ, and V defined as follows (B. Liu, 2011, p. 243):

- $U = [U_1, U_2, ..., U_r]$ is an orthonormal matrix of dimension $m \times r$, i.e. $U^T * U = I_r$ (identity matrix), and the value r is the rank of the matrix A. The columns of the matrix U, which are referred to as *left singular vectors*, are eigenvectors corresponding to the non-negative eigenvalues of the matrix $A*A^T$.

- $\Sigma = diag(\sigma_1, \sigma_2, ..., \sigma_r)$ is a diagonal matrix of dimension $r \times r$. The diagonal elements $\sigma 1$, $\sigma 2$, ..., σ_r are referred to as *singular values*, and the following relation between them is true: $\sigma_1 \geq \sigma_2 \geq ... \geq \sigma_r > 0$. These singular values are the square roots of the non-negative eigenvalues of $A*A^T$.

- $V = [V_1, V_2, ..., V_n]$ is an orthonormal matrix of dimension $r \times n$, i.e. $V^T * V = I_n$. The columns of the matrix V, which are referred to as *right singular vectors*, are eigenvectors corresponding to the non-negative eigenvalues of the matrix $A^T * A$.

4 Experimental Results

The user interface of the application is presented in Figure 1. The interface contains three major discernible areas that provide visual representation of the sentiments expressed by both human and bot.

The left zone is designed to allow interaction between human and bot, users can either input different opinions about subjects or query the system for information. Questions and answers are sorted according to a timestamp maintained by the chat area.

The evolution of sentiments for both bot and human are visible in the center and left area of the interface (the plotted data includes results from all the lexicons discussed in the previous section).

As the conversation progresses, the main focus is to have a high increase of the influence score. As such, alongside the presented components, the application contains an area where one can view the influence score exerted by the chat bot.

The metric used to measure the influence score is based on the sentiments calculated for the questions. We take into consideration only positive and negative sentiment questions. The influence score is calculated as the ratio of the number of positive sentiment questions and the sum between the number of positive sentiment questions and number of negative sentiment question:

$$\frac{\#\text{ of positive questions}}{\#\text{ of positive questions} + \#\text{ of negative questions}}$$

5 Conclusions

Communication constitutes the core element of human interactions and recently also between humans and computers. However, communicating means not only giving or receiving information, but also the ability to influence one another's beliefs.

In this paper, we presented a question answering system in order to integrate a module to analyze opinion influence. A human is influenced by a bot in a conversation if he changes his initial opinion. More precisely, the user inputs more and more questions with positive sentiments over time. The results show that this is possible.

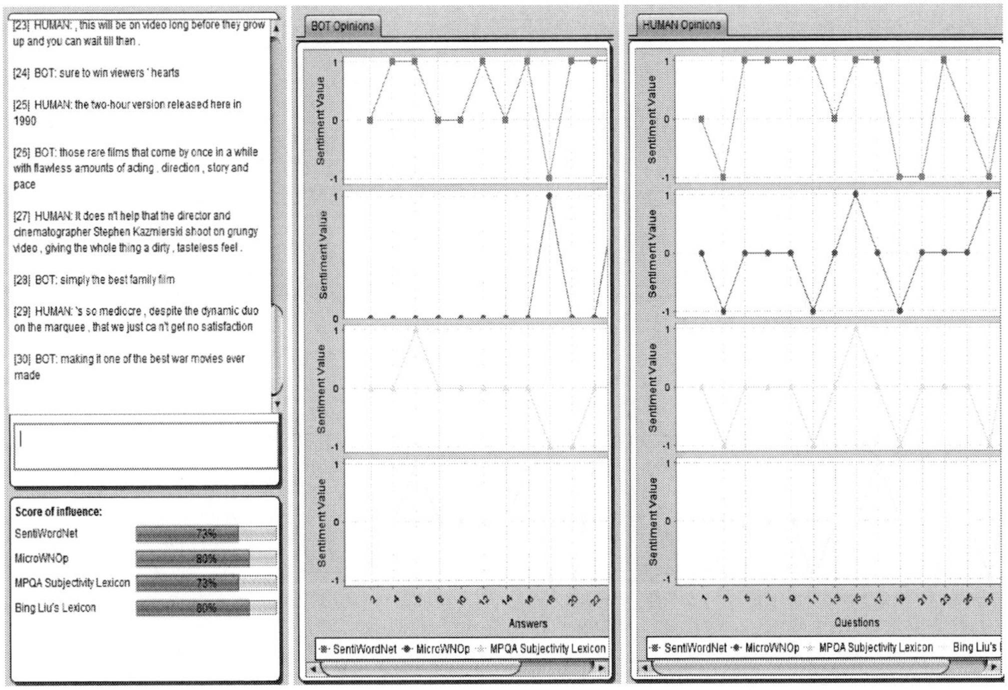

Figure 1: Interface for the oIQa framework.

Acknowledgments

This work has been funded by University Politehnica of Bucharest, through the "Excellence Research Grants" Program, UPB – GEX. Identifier: UPB–EXCELENTA–2016, Contract number 11/30.09.2016.

References

Ashton Anderson, Daniel Huttenlocher, Jon Kleinberg, and Jure Leskovec. 2012. Discovering value from community activity on focused question answering sites: a case study of stack overflow. *In Proceedings of the 18th International Conference on Knowledge Discovery and Data Mining*, pages 850–858.

Alexandra Balahur, Ester Boldrini, Andres Montoyo, and Patricio Martínez-Barco. 2009a. Opinion and generic question answering systems: a performance analysis. In *Proceedings of the ACL-IJCNLP 2009 conference short papers*, pages 157–160.

Alexandra Balahur, Mijail Alexandrov Kabadjov, Josef Steinberger, Ralf Steinberger, and Andrés Montoyo. 2009b. Summarizing Opinions in Blog Threads. In *Proceedings of PACLIC*, pages 606-613.

Dumitru C. Cercel, and Stefan Trausan-Matu. 2014a. Opinion Influence Analysis in Online Forum Threads. In *Proceedings of Symbolic and Numeric Algorithms for Scientific Computing (SYNASC)*, pages 228-235.

Dumitru C. Cercel and Stefan Trausan-Matu. 2014b. User-Level Opinion Propagation Analysis in Discussion Forum Threads. In *Proceedings of Artificial Intelligence: Methodology, Systems, and Applications*, pages 25-36.

Sabrina Cerini, Valentina Compagnoni, Alice Demontis, Maicol Formentelli, and G. Gandini. 2007. Micro-WNOp: A gold standard for the evaluation of automatically compiled lexical resources for opinion mining. In *A. Sans (Ed.), Language resources and linguistic theory: Typology, second language acquisition, English linguistics: Franco Angeli Editore.*

Andrea Esuli, Stefano Baccianella, and Fabrizio Sebastiani. 2010. SentiWordNet 3.0: An Enhanced Lexical Resource for Sentiment Analysis and Opinion Mining. In *Proceedings of the Seventh conference on International Language Resources and Evaluation (LREC'10)*, Valletta, Malta.

Christiane Fellbaum. 1998. WordNet: An Electronic Lexical Database. Cambridge, MA: MIT Press.

Minqing Hu, and Bing Liu. 2004. Mining and summarizing customer reviews. In *Proceedings of the tenth ACM SIGKDD international conference on Knowledge discovery and data mining*, Seattle, WA, USA, pages 168-177.

Jihie Kim, Jae-Bong Yoo, Ho Lim, Huida Qiu, Zornitsa Kozareva, and Aram Galstyan. 2013. Sentiment Prediction Using Collaborative Filtering. In *Proceedings of ICWSM.*

Thomas K. Landauer, Peter W Foltz, and Darrell Laham. 1998. An introduction to latent semantic analysis. *Discourse processes*, 25(2-3), 259-284.

Bing Liu. 2011. Web Data Mining Exploring Hyperlinks, Contents and Usage Data: Springer-Verlag.

Lu Liu, Jie Tang, Jiawei Han, Meng Jiang, and Shiqiang Yang. 2010. Mining topic-level influence in heterogeneous networks. In *Proceedings of the 19th ACM international conference on Information and knowledge management*, Toronto, ON, Canada, pages 199-208.

Marie-Catherine De Marneffe, Bill MacCartney, and Christopher D Manning. 2006. Generating typed dependency parses from phrase structure parses. In *Proceedings of LREC*, pages 449-454.

Marie-Catherine De Marneffe, and Christopher Manning. 2008. Stanford typed dependencies manual.

Julian McAuley and Alex Yang. 2016. Addressing complex and subjective product-related queries with customer reviews. In *Proceedings of the 25th International Conference on World Wide Web,* pages 625–635.

Amit Mishra and Sanjay K. Jain. 2016. A survey on question answering systems with Classification. *Journal of King Saud University-Computer and Information Sciences.* 28(3): 345–361.

Richard Socher, Alex Perelygin, Jean Y. Wu, Jason Chuang Christopher D. Manning, Andrew Y. Ng and Christopher Potts. 2013. Recursive deep models for semantic compositionality over a sentiment treebank. In *Proceedings of the conference on empirical methods in natural language processing EMNLP (Volume 1631).*

Jie Tang, Sen Wu, and Jimeng Sun. 2013. Confluence: conformity influence in large social networks. In *Proceedings of the 19th ACM SIGKDD international conference on Knowledge discovery and data mining*, Chicago, Illinois, USA, pages 347-355.

Jie Tang, Jimeng Sun, Chi Wang, and Zi Yang. 2009. Social influence analysis in large-scale networks. In *Proceedings of the 15th ACM SIGKDD international conference on Knowledge discovery and data mining*, Paris, France, pages 807-816.

Mengting Wan and Julian McAuley. 2016. Modeling ambiguity, subjectivity, and diverging viewpoints in opinion question answering systems. In *Proceedings of the International Conference on Data Mining (ICDM)*, pages 489–498.

Theresa Wilson, Janyce Wiebe, and Paul Hoffmann. 2005. Recognizing contextual polarity in phrase-level sentiment analysis. In *Proceedings of the conference on Human Language Technology and Empirical Methods in Natural Language Processing*, Vancouver, British Columbia, Canada, pages 347-354.

Man.-C. Yuen, Irwin King, and Kwong -S. Leung. 2011. A survey of crowdsourcing systems. In *Proceedings of Privacy, Security, Risk and Trust (PASSAT) and 2011 IEEE Third International Conference on Social Computing (SocialCom), 2011 IEEE Third International Conference on*, pages. 766–773.

Automatic Summarization of Online Debates

Nattapong Sanchan, Ahmet Aker and **Kalina Bontcheva**

Natural Language Processing Group, Department of Computer Science,
The University of Sheffield, 211 Portobello, Sheffield, United Kingdom
{nsanchan1, ahmet.aker, k.bontcheva}@sheffield.ac.uk
`https://www.sheffield.ac.uk/dcs`

Abstract

Debate summarization is one of the novel and challenging research areas in automatic text summarization which has been largely unexplored. In this paper, we develop a debate summarization pipeline to summarize key topics which are discussed or argued in the two opposing sides of online debates. We view that the generation of debate summaries can be achieved by clustering, cluster labeling, and visualization. In our work, we investigate two different clustering approaches for the generation of the summaries. In the first approach, we generate the summaries by applying purely term-based clustering and cluster labeling. The second approach makes use of X-means for clustering and Mutual Information for labeling the clusters. Both approaches are driven by ontologies. We visualize the results using bar charts. We think that our results are a smooth entry for users aiming to receive the first impression about what is discussed within a debate topic containing waste number of argumentations.

1 Introduction

As the number of Internet users has been growing significantly, information is published and stored digitally in textual forms. Online debate is one example of the information which has been massively published. As more and more debate content increases, it becomes a difficult task to easily and quickly discover key arguments that are expressed in the vast amount of debate data. Automatic Text Summarization can help users to extract or summarize those key arguments more efficiently and reduce the reading time.

Online debate forums normally contain two sides of debates: proponent and opponent. This structure gives opportunities for users to choose a stance (side) for a debate topic, expresses their opinions to support their propositions, and opposes other propositions. In this paper, we explore online debates which are related to the existence of global warming. A side of proponents believes in the existence of global warming and the other side, the opponents, says that global warming is not true. When the proponents and the opponents express their sentiments, opinions, and pieces of evidence to support their propositions, arguments between them arise.

In this paper we aim to summarize online debates about global warming. In our approach we first extract salient sentences from the two opposing sides of debates (i.e. arguments published by users). Next, we cluster them by some sort of similarity. For clustering we investigate two different approaches. Our first approach is a term-based clustering approach. The second approach is based on flat clustering, namely X-means, which can automatically determine the number of clusters. Ontologies are used as the backbone for both approaches. Ontologies have been used broadly in automatic text summarization studies. However, to the best of our knowledge, this approach has not yet been applied for summarizing online debates, especially when our purpose is to capture arguments conversed in both opposing sides. Once clusters are generated, labels representing the clusters are extracted. Again we follow two approaches. The first approach is a simple one and selects as a label an ontological term that is shared by all salient sentences within the cluster. The second labeling approach extracts such a term, based on Mutual Information (MI). The resulting clusters along with their labels are visualized using bar charts. Our results show that clustering with

Proceedings of Natural Language Processing and Information Retrieval Workshop, pages 19–27,
Varna, Bulgaria, Sep 7 2017.

X-means and label generation using MI is a better choice for the purpose of online debates summarization.

The rest of the paper is organized as follows. Section 2 discusses about related work in online debate summarization. The online debate data related to the existence of global warming are elaborated in Section 3. Section 4 illustrates the system structure for developing our debate summarization system. Within the same section we also present our evaluation results. We conclude in 5.

2 Related Work

Debate summarization is one of the novel research areas in automatic text summarization which has been largely unexplored (Ranade et al., 2013). Examples of related work in debate summarization includes *Contrastive Summarization*, *Comparative Summarization*, and *Debate Stance Recognition*. Contrastive Summarization is the study of generating summary for two entities and finding the difference in sentiments among them (Lerman and McDonald, 2009). This kind of summarization requires the classification of polarity in order to *contrast* opinions expressed in different sentiments (Campr and Jezek, 2012; Paul et al., 2010). Kim and Zhai (2009) summarized contrastive pairs of sentences by aligning positive and negative opinions on the same aspect. In this work, contrastive sentence pairs were constructed based on two criteria: 1) choose sentences that represent a major sentiment orientation; and 2) the two sentences should have opposite opinions on the same aspect. Similarity functions were used for determining contrastive sentence pairs. Then sentence pairs were used as input for generating the final summary. The summary was aimed to help readers compare the pros and cons of mixed opinions.

Comparative Summarization aims to find the difference between two comparable entities so that sentiment classification may not be required (Campr and Jezek, 2012). Zhai et al. (2004) worked on comparative text mining problem which aimed to discover common topics in news articles and laptop reviews and to summarize commonalities and differences in a given set of comparable text collections. A probabilistic mixture model was proposed. It generates clusters of topics across all collections and in each collection of document. The model generates k collections of specific topics for each collection and k common topics across all collections. Each topic is characterized by multinomial word distribution (also called a unigram language model). High probability words were used as representatives of each cluster and are also included in the summary.

Debate Stance Recognition aims to detect stance of an opinion's holder in text. Somasundaran and Wiebe (2009) noticed that in online debate posts, people debate issues, express their favorites, oppose other stances, and argue why their thoughts are correct. To determine positive sentiment about one target, expressing negative sentiment about the other side is a key target. For instance, in a debate "*Which mobile phone is better: iPhone VS Blackberry?*", people supporting iPhone may give reasons to affirm why iPhone is better. In addition, they also express why Blackberry is not. On the Blackberry side, people may also find reasons to support their opinions and argue why the phone is unfavorable. Therefore, to identify stance, it is important to not only consider positive and negative sentiment, but also consider which target an opinion refers to.

Unlike these, the study of Ranade et al. (2013) directly tackled debate summarization problem and it is the one which is closest to our work. In that work, system summaries are extracted by ranking the smallest units of debates, called Dialogue Acts (DAs). The ranking of sentences is based on features including, words in DAs that is co-occurring in debate topic, topics with opinions expressed on it, sentence position, and sentence length features. However, this work does not explicitly highlight what is the key content to be summarized and how the debate summary is presented. This is different to our work. On the other hand, in our work, we highlight the summarization of key content in debates and visualize them to be easily accessed by users.

3 Online Debate Data

In our earlier work we created freely available debate dataset on climate change domain[1], also referred as Salient Sentence Selection Dataset (SSSD). Each debate consists of two opposing sides, *Agree* and *Disagree*. Whereas the opinion on the *Agree* side believes that global warming exists, the *Disagree* side opposes this opinion. In this dataset, each debate comment was manually anno-

[1]This dataset can be downloaded at `https://goo.gl/3aicDN`.

tated by 5 judgments. The aim of the annotation was to select from each comment 20% sentences that were salient and worth for inclusion in a summary. For instance, for a comment containing 10 sentences 2 sentences were extracted by each annotator. The dataset contains 11 debate topics with 341 comments in total. Average number of comments for a topic is 31 comments, with the minimum and maximum of 5 and 103 comments respectively.

4 Framework

To generate a bar chart representing a summary of an online debate topic we proposed a pipeline with two branches where each branch presents either a term-based clustering and the term-based labeling method or X-means based clustering and the MI labeling strategy. The flow of the pipeline is shown in Figure 1. The system assumes an input of n comments from the agree and disagree sides. Each comment consists of several sentences. We aim to select the most salient sentences from each comment, cluster the salient sentences according to their content similarity, generate clusters representing labels, and finally visualize the results using a bar chart summary. In the following sections we introduce each of the components and provide evaluation results.

4.1 Automatic Salient Sentence Selection

For the shown pipeline in Figure 1 we used an extractive automatic summarization system reported in our earlier work.[2] There are 8 main features defined in this system. Those features include sentence position (SP), sentence length (SL), title words (TT), the presence of conjunctive adverbs (CJ), cosine similarity of topic signatures[3] and sentences (COS_TPS), cosine similarity of climate change terms[4] and sentences (COS_CCTS), cosine similarity of sentence and title words (COS_TTS), and the semantic similarity of sentence and title words (COS_STT) using Doc2Vec. Additionally, we also investigated the Combination of features (CB) in the salient sentence selection. For a given comment the system extracts 20% sentences from it that are deemed as salient.

4.1.1 Evaluation

We used ROUGE-1, ROUGE-2, and ROUGE-SU4 evaluation metrics to evaluate the quality of the system summaries, i.e. the selection of salient sentences. As reference summaries we used the manually generated summaries from the freely available dataset, SSSD. Our results revealed that sentence position outperforms other features indicating that the most salient sentences are always. In addition, other useful key features are debate title words feature, and cosine similarity of debate title words and sentences feature. The complete set of results are shown in Table 1.

4.2 Term-Based Clustering

To perform clustering we used terms extracted through ontologies. We employed the English ClimaPinion service[5] from the DecarboNet project[6] as the background knowledge to capture climate change topics and extract from each salient sentence topical terms. To obtain clusters we grouped sentences containing the same label within the same cluster. If a sentence contained more than one term then it was assigned to several groups allowing the sentence to be soft-clustered.[7] Also note, terms with the same semantic meaning can be expressed differently. To address this, for each label, we obtained a list of its synonyms from WordNet (Miller, 1995). If the labels shared common synonyms, we considered they are the same labels. Consequentially, the sentences automatically annotated with such labels were merged to the same clusters.

4.2.1 Evaluation

The evaluation of the ontology based term extraction has been evaluated somewhere else. By consisting of two environmental ontologies, GEMET (GEneral Multilingual Environmental Thesaurus) and Reegle, the ClimaPinion yields great results in recognizing environmental terms in text, with the precision, recall, and F1 measure of 85.87%, 53.05%, and 65.58% respectively (Maynard and Bontcheva, 2015).

The results derived from the term-based clustering approach are evaluated with the Silhouette index (Rousseeuw, 1987). Silhouette evaluates

[2]https://goo.gl/xqVeJf.

[3]We used an approach described by (Lin and Hovy, 2000) to obtain a list of topic signatures. We extract the topic signatures from our dataset which is related to climate change.

[4]The terms are obtained by aggregating document keywords from online news media coverage on climate change.

[5]http://services.gate.ac.uk/decarbonet/sentiment/

[6]https://www.decarbonet.eu

[7]Within a cluster all sentences must share one particular term but each sentence may contain other terms that are not shared by other sentences within the same cluster.

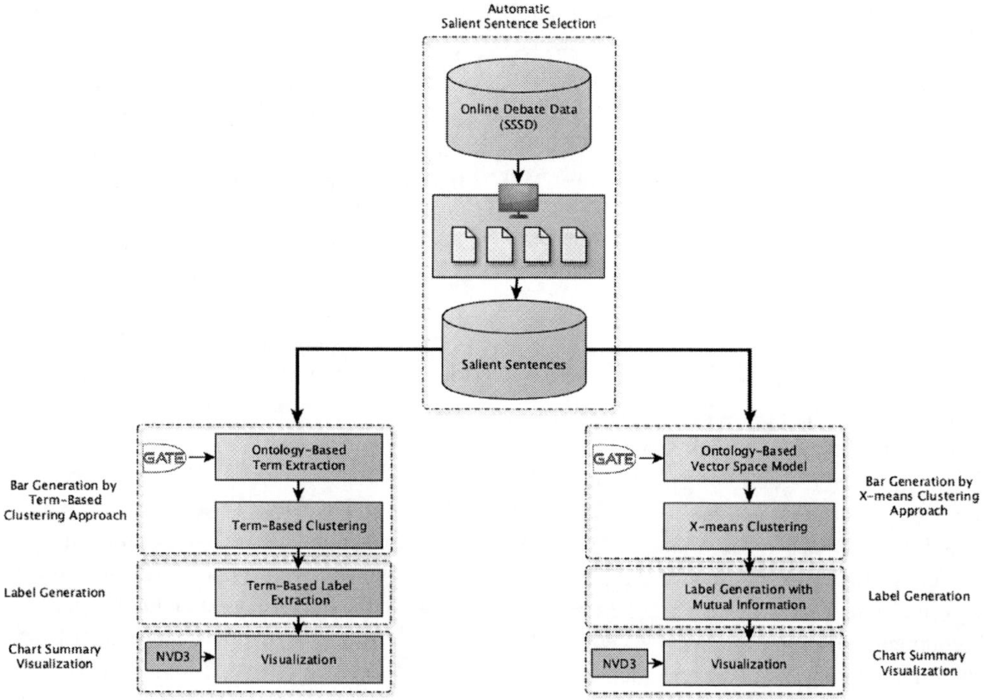

Figure 1: The framework for generating the Chart Summary for online debate summarization

ROUGE-N	CB	CJ	COS_CCT	COS_TTS	COS_TPS	SL	SP	COS_STT	TT
R-1	0.4773	0.4988	0.3389	0.5630	0.3907	0.4307	**0.6124**	0.4304	0.5407
R-2	0.3981	0.4346	0.2558	0.5076	0.2986	0.3550	**0.5375**	0.3561	0.4693
R-SU4	0.3783	0.4147	0.2340	0.4780	0.2699	0.3335	**0.4871**	0.3340	0.4303

Table 1: ROUGE scores derived from each feature in the Salient Sentence Selection task

Table 2: Average silhouette scores derived from the term-based clustering approach

Number of Clusters	Average Silhouette Score
39	0.0000

the clustering performance by determining the appropriateness of documents assigned to a cluster rather than the other clusters. These documents are represented as coordinates. Silhouette calculates the pairwise difference in both inter-cluster and intra-cluster distance. We calculated an average silhouette score and reported it in Table 2. As shown in the table, the system generated 39 clusters based on the climate change terms annotated by the ClimaPinion service. It achieved the silhouette score around zero, similar to the work presented by Wang and Koopman (2017). The interpretation based on the score is the data points are assigned nearly to the decision boundaries of the clusters. Especially, when salient sentences contain multiple climate change topics, clear clustering boundaries are difficult to achieve. This circumstance indicates that such a simple clustering approach is less applicable for grouping semantically similar sentences together and that the task asks for more sophisticated ways for achieving a better performance. We will discuss an alternative solution in Section 4.4.

4.3 Term-Based Label Extraction

After grouping salient sentences together, the groups or clusters should be given labels which clearly reflect the content in the clusters (Aker et al., 2016). Similar to the clustering approach, where we grouped salient sentences by the ontological term they share, we used the sharing term as the label to represent the cluster. This is based on the assumption that the climate change terms which are annotated in the sentences do already elaborate the central meaning of the clusters.

4.3.1 Evaluation

In the labeling evaluation, we compared the system labels against the baseline labels. We generated the baseline labels by applying *tf*idf*. It is a common approach in most information retrieval systems (Ponte and Croft, 1998) which consists of two main components, *tf* and *idf*. In our experiment, *tf* indicates the frequency of terms occurs in a cluster[8]. *idf* presents the number clusters in which the term occurs. These components allow us to reduce common terms in the clusters and discover more discriminative terms having fairly low term frequency in the clusters. To determine the candidate labels, we calculated the score for each term by the multiplication of *tf* and *idf*. The term with the top score was chosen as the cluster label.

In the evaluation of cluster labels, we followed the manual evaluation method presented by Aker et al. (2016). We invited three participants, two PhD candidates and one researcher having background in Computer Science, to evaluate the labels. The evaluation was presented as an online form. The participants were asked to read the sentences in the given clusters and score the labels. The baseline and system labels were shown in random order. For each label, the participants were asked to answer five-point Likert scale questions, ranking from *strongly disagree* (1) to *strongly agree* (5). The questions include i) Question 1: By reading the label, I can understand it, ii) Question 2: This label is a complete phrase, and iii) Question 3: This label precisely reflects the content of the sentences in cluster. Along with the three questions, we presented 13 clusters with a maximum of 10 salient sentences (so that the participants are able to read the content prior to the labeling evaluation) and a minimum of 2 salient sentences. Figure 2 illustrates the results of the labeling evaluation.

As we can see from the figure, in overall, the quality of system labels outperforms the baseline labels. In Q1, the system labels compared to the baseline labels are more understandable with the average score of 4.59 and 3.33 respectively. Likewise, in Q2, the system labels are more completed phrases than the baseline with the mean difference of 1.51. Lastly, with the average preference

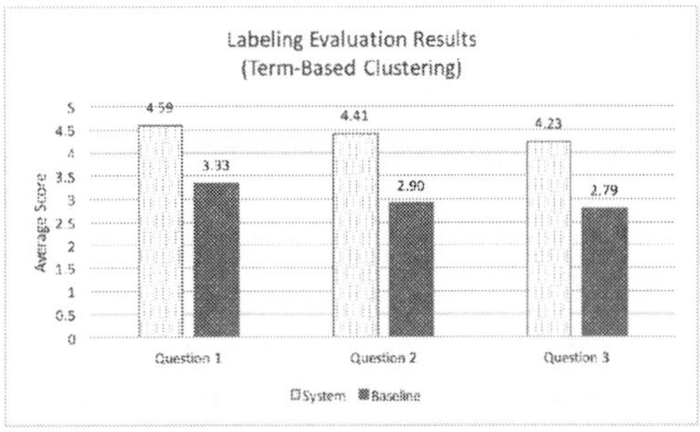

Figure 2: The labeling evaluation performed on the term-based clustering approach. The average preference scores generated by 3 participants on a scale 1: strongly disagree to 5: strongly agree

scores of 4.23 in Q3, the system labels are more reflecting the quality of content in the clusters than those generated by the baseline having the score of 2.79. Additionally, the quality of the system labels is further confirmed by a statistical significance analysis with Mann-Whitney U Test. The test reveals that significance difference is found in the system labels ($Md_{Q1-Q3} = 5$, $n_{Q1-Q3} = 39$) and the baseline labels ($Md_{Q1} = 4$, $Md_{Q2} = 3$, $Md_{Q3} = 2$), $U_{Q1} = 363$, $U_{Q2} = 343$, $U_{Q3} = 386$, $z_{Q1} = -4.25$, $z_{Q2} = -4.36$, $z_{Q3} = -3.92$, $p < 0.01$, $r_{Q1} = 0.48$, $r_{Q2} = 0.49$, $r_{Q3} = 0.44$. We also measured the inter-annotator agreement using Krippendorffs alpha coefficient[9]. The agreement in Q1, Q2, and Q3 are 0.31, 0.27, and 0.35 respectively.

4.4 X-means Clustering

In Section 4.2 we have shown that the idea of performing clustering based on shared terms results in poor clustering performance. The approach leads to too many clusters which are very close to each other. In this section we aim to overcome the problem of poor performance of the term-based clustering approach and use X-means (Pelleg and Moore, 2000), an extended version of K-means, to cluster the salient sentences selected by the summarization system. One of the benefits of X-means is that it is able to automatically detect the number of clusters. By computing the Bayesian Information Criterion (BIC) scores, X-means decides if cluster centroids should be split. We applied ontology-based vector space model approach

[8]Since sentences can carry more than a term it is likely that a cluster has several climate change terms.

[9]The measurement is performed using *nltk metrics*, http://www.nltk.org/api/nltk.metrics.html.

to create vectors as the similarity inputs for X-means.

4.4.1 Similarity Measurement

To enable X-means to process the clustering, a similarity needs to be defined to determine which sentences are close to each other. In the definition of our similarity measurement, the automatic selected salient sentences are transformed into vectors using the Vector Space Model (VSM). In the document indexing stage, we employed the ontologies to automatically annotate key climate change terms in the SSSD. The employment of ontology-based approach benefits the transformation of words to vectors by help capturing relevance of specific topics. We derived 64 significant climate change topics. Term frequency was counted for each term to generate vectors for each sentence. To generate a similarity matrix, cosine similarity measure was used to calculate cosine similarity scores among the vectors. After the similarity matrix was constructed, we applied a Principal Component Analysis (PCA)[10] for the dimensionality reduction.

4.4.2 Evaluation

Similar to the ontology term-based clustering we evaluated the results of the X-means clustering using Silhouette index. Results are reported in Table 3.

As shown in the table, the average silhouette score is derived from the calculation based on the similarity definition obtained by the ontology-based vector space model. We achieved a high silhouette score of 0.9878, with the total number of 19 generated clusters. A silhouette close to 1.0 indicates good cohesion and separation of the clustering results, meaning that the average distance from a coordinate in a cluster to the other coordinates within its own cluster is less than the average distance to all coordinate in the nearest cluster. In addition, when the score is close to 0, the coordinates in the clusters are nearly close or on the decision boundary between two neighbouring clusters. A negative silhouette score is obtained when coordinates might be assigned to wrong clusters. In other words, the coordinates are very close to the neighbouring cluster rather than the coordinates in their own clusters (Rousseeuw, 1987). In our experiment, we concluded that the clustering results obtained by X-means clustering algorithm have strong clustering structure and is more appropriate for the task of summarizing debate data.

Table 3: Average silhouette scores derived from X-means clustering results

Number of Clusters	Average Silhouette Score
19	0.9878

4.5 Label Generation with Mutual Information

To generate labels from the X-means clusters we could have followed the same approach as described in Section 4.3, namely picking up a term that is shared by all or majority of the salient sentences within a cluster. We tried this however, to our surprise the performance was very low compared to what we achieved in Section 4.3. Nevertheless this helped us to draw two conclusions. First, the performance in Section 4.3 is high because the labels were so selected that all salient sentences within a group shared that label. Second the size of the clusters was not big so that the label had high chance to be representative of the cluster. This pictures changed once the cluster size increased and also the salient sentences covered several different climate change terms. Because of this selecting a label was not about just simply selecting the term that appears in all or majority of the salient sentences. We used Mutual Information (MI) to make this decision for us.

MI is a prevalent feature selection approach that involves in the calculation of a utility measure A(*t*,*c*). MI quantifies how much information that term *t* contributing to the correct classification judgment on class *c* (Manning et al., 2008). The MI formula is shown in Equation 1, where U is a random variable that holds the value e_t. If a sentence contains term *t*, the value of e_t is *1*. Otherwise, the e_t is 0. C is a random variable that holds the value e_c. The value of e_c is 1 indicating that a sentence is in class *c* and it is 0 if it is not.

[10]sklearn.decomposition.PCA: https://goo.gl/QqiWec

$$I(U;C) = \sum_{e_t \in \{1,0\}} \sum_{e_c \in \{1,0\}} P(U = e_t, C = e_c) \log_2 \frac{P(U = e_t, C = e_c)}{P(U = e_t)P(C = e_c)'} \quad (1)$$

$$I(U;C) = \frac{N_{11}}{N} \log_2 \frac{NN_{11}}{N_{1.}N_{.1}} + \frac{N_{01}}{N} \log_2 \frac{NN_{01}}{N_{0.}N_{.1}} + \frac{N_{10}}{N} \log_2 \frac{NN_{10}}{N_{1.}N_{.0}} + \frac{N_{00}}{N} \log_2 \frac{NN_{00}}{N_{0.}N_{.0}} \quad (2)$$

To calculate the mutual information scores for candidate terms, we applied the maximum likelihood estimation of probability as shown in Equation 2 (Manning et al., 2008). From the equation, *N* refers to the counts of sentences in which its subscripts take the values of e_t and e_c. For instance, N_{01} refers to the number of sentences that do not containing term t ($e_t = 1$) but in class c ($ec = 1$). $N_{1.}$ is derived from the addition of N_{10} and N_{11}. *N* refers to the total number of sentences. In each cluster, we calculated the score of each candidate term. The term with the higher MI score was selected as the cluster label for that cluster.

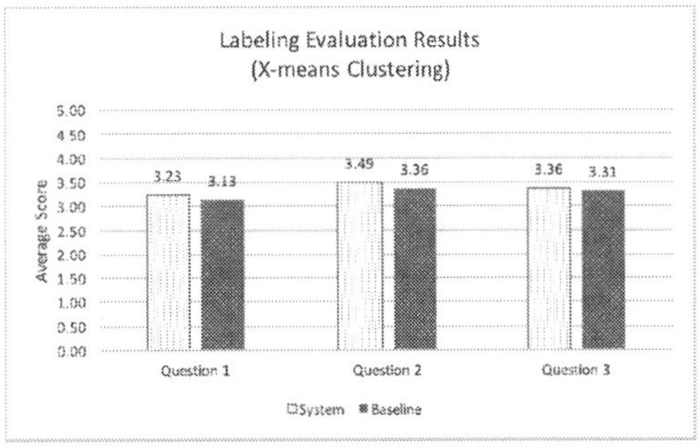

Figure 3: The labeling evaluation performed on the X-means clustering approach. The average preference scores generated by 3 participants on a scale 1: strongly disagree to 5: strongly agree

4.5.1 Labeling Evaluation

In order to evaluate the system labels generated by the results derived from X-means clustering approach, we applied the same evaluation procedure as well the baseline discussed in Section 4.3.1. The results are illustrated in Figure 2. As can be seen from the figure, the average preference scores of the system outperform the baseline. In Q1, the system labels are more understandable than the baseline, with the mean difference of 0.10. In Q2, the system labels more completed phrases than the baseline labels, with a higher mean score of 0.13. Lastly, in Q3, the system labels are still better than the baseline labels with the mean difference of 0.05. The system labels are more meaningful for presenting the central meaning of the content in the clusters. However, as there is a slight difference between the results of the system labels and baseline labels, Mann-Whitney U test reveals that no significant difference, with the z values of -0.705,-0.427, and -0.389, with the significance levels of p= 0.481, 0.670, and 0.697 respectively. The values of Krippendorff's alpha, by another three participants, for Q1, Q2, and Q3 are 0.33, 0.44, and 0.56 respectively.

4.6 Visualization

Sanchan et al. (2016) have manually investigated various representation models for displaying or visualizing summaries of online debates. Unlike traditional summaries, the debates extracts have to capture main concepts discussed in both sides and enable the reader to look at those concepts from both proponent and opponent sites. The authors proposed the Chart Summary which presents the clusters by bars. Each bar is marked with the cluster label. In this work we adopt the Chart Summary for visualization purposes. An example Chart Summary is shown in Figure 4.

In the generation of the bars in Chart Summary, the bars are the clusters that express related content in both opposing sides. Therefore, it is important to match clusters from the two opposing sides which express the related content. We call this approach as *alignment*. From the two opposing sides, we align the clusters based on the cluster labels. The clusters sharing mutual labels are aligned. For alignment, we used cosine similarity over vector spaces representing the labels. The vector also contains semantically related words enriched from WordNet. Clusters which have no pair will not be aligned and thus will not be presented in the Chart Summary. Once the pairs of aligned clusters are derived, we count the number of salient sentences in those clusters, separately in each opposing side. Those numbers represent the frequencies of the bars.

After all components of a Chart Summary are completely generated, they are exported to NVD3 JAVA script[11] for the purpose of visualizing the Chart Summary. Figure 4 illustrates a Chart Summary for the online debates data which runs on a web browser[12].

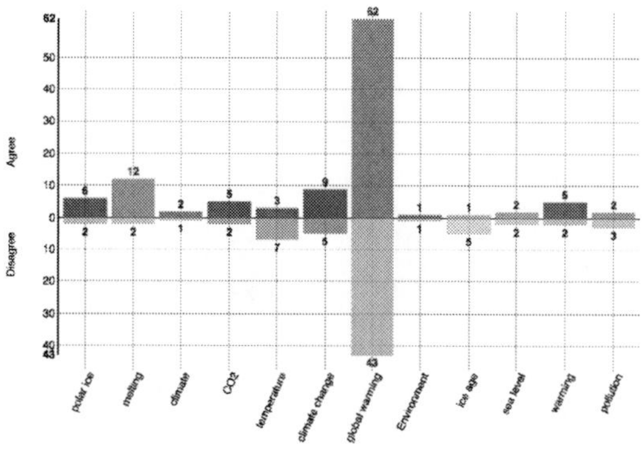

Figure 4: Chart Summary for Debate Data

5 Conclusion

In this paper, we investigated one of the novel and challenging problems in automatic text summarization of online debates and proposed a framework to tackle this problem. We aimed to generate Chart Summaries which represent the high-level topics of online debates. The Chart Summary is composed of three main components, including the bars, labels, and frequencies of the bars. We proposed an ontological term-based driven clustering and cluster labeling pipeline to guide the debate summary generation. In our approach we used an online service to automatically annotate climate change terms in salient sentences and to group related salient sentences into the same cluster. For clustering we investigated two variants both making use of ontological terms. The first, a simply approach, groups salient sentences by shared terms. The second approach applies X-means clustering. The evaluation has shown that the X-means approach is a better choice for clustering. We create labels to represent each cluster. Again here we investigated two different approaches both making use of ontological terms. The first approach, again a simply one, labels each cluster with the term shared by all members within the cluster. The second approach picks up the best term according to Mutual Information. The manual evaluation showed that the simple approach achieves higher results than the MI one. However, as discussed the simply approach achieved high results because of the size of the clusters and led to poor results when the size of the cluster grew which is the case with the X-means clustering. Once the clusters and labels are generated with align the pro and contra parts and visualize the results using NVD3.

In future work we plan to enrich the Chart Summary with additional details such as enabling the users to see example debates for each pair of clusters.

[11] http://nvd3.org

[12] A full version of Chart Summary can be accessed via https://goo.gl/wjBh7V.

References

Ahmet Aker, Monica Lestari Paramita, Emina Kurtic, Adam Funk, Emma Barker, Mark Hepple, and Robert J. Gaizauskas. 2016. Automatic label generation for news comment clusters. In *INLG 2016 - Proceedings of the Ninth International Natural Language Generation Conference, September 5-8, 2016, Edinburgh, UK*. pages 61–69. http://aclweb.org/anthology/W/W16/W16-6610.pdf.

Michal Campr and Karel Jezek. 2012. Comparative summarization via latent semantic analysis. In *Lastest Trends in Information Technology;Proceedings of the 1st WSEAS International Conference on Information Technology and Computer Networks (ITCN '12), Proceedings of the 1st WSEAS International Conference on Cloud Computing (CLC '12), Proceedings of the 1st WSEAS International Conference on Programming Languages and Compilers (PRLC '12)*. WSEAS Press, Stroudsburg, PA, USA, Recent Advances in Computer Engineering Series 7, pages 279–284. http://textmining.zcu.cz/publications/wseas-mcampr.pdf.

Hyun Duk Kim and ChengXiang Zhai. 2009. Generating comparative summaries of contradictory opinions in text. In David Wai-Lok Cheung, Il-Yeol Song, Wesley W. Chu, Xiaohua Hu, and Jimmy J. Lin, editors, *CIKM*. ACM, pages 385–394. http://dblp.uni-trier.de/db/conf/cikm/cikm2009.html.

Kevin Lerman and Ryan McDonald. 2009. Contrastive summarization: An experiment with consumer reviews. In *Proceedings of Human Language Technologies: The 2009 Annual Conference of the North American Chapter of the Association for Computational Linguistics, Companion Volume: Short Papers*. Association for Computational Linguistics, Stroudsburg,

PA, USA, NAACL-Short '09, pages 113–116. http://dl.acm.org/citation.cfm?id=1620853.1620886.

Chin-Yew Lin and Eduard Hovy. 2000. The automated acquisition of topic signatures for text summarization. In *Proceedings of the 18th Conference on Computational Linguistics - Volume 1*. Association for Computational Linguistics, Stroudsburg, PA, USA, COLING '00, pages 495–501. https://doi.org/10.3115/990820.990892.

C. D. Manning, P. Raghavan, and H. Schtze. 2008. *Introduction to Information Retrieval*. Cambridge University Press. http://www-csli.stanford.edu/ hinrich/information-retrieval-book.html.

Diana Maynard and Kalina Bontcheva. 2015. Understanding climate change tweets: an open source toolkit for social media analysis. In Volker Wohlgemuth Chris Preist Elina Eriksson Vivian Kvist Johannsen, Stefan Jensen, editor, *Atlantis Press*. Morgan Kaufmann Publishers Inc., Atlantis Press, pages 242–250.

George A Miller. 1995. Wordnet: a lexical database for english. *Communications of the ACM* 38(11):39–41.

Michael J Paul, ChengXiang Zhai, and Roxana Girju. 2010. Summarizing contrastive viewpoints in opinionated text. In *Proceedings of the 2010 Conference on Empirical Methods in Natural Language Processing*. Association for Computational Linguistics, pages 66–76.

Dan Pelleg and Andrew W. Moore. 2000. X-means: Extending k-means with efficient estimation of the number of clusters. In *Proceedings of the Seventeenth International Conference on Machine Learning*. Morgan Kaufmann Publishers Inc., San Francisco, CA, USA, ICML '00, pages 727–734. http://dl.acm.org/citation.cfm?id=645529.657808.

Jay M. Ponte and W. Bruce Croft. 1998. A language modeling approach to information retrieval. In *Proceedings of the 21st Annual International ACM SIGIR Conference on Research and Development in Information Retrieval*. ACM, New York, NY, USA, SIGIR '98, pages 275–281. https://doi.org/10.1145/290941.291008.

Sarvesh Ranade, Jayant Gupta, Vasudeva Varma, and Radhika Mamidi. 2013. Online debate summarization using topic directed sentiment analysis. In *Proceedings of the Second International Workshop on Issues of Sentiment Discovery and Opinion Mining*. ACM, New York, NY, USA, WISDOM '13, pages 7:1–7:6. https://doi.org/10.1145/2502069.2502076.

Peter Rousseeuw. 1987. Silhouettes: A graphical aid to the interpretation and validation of cluster analysis. *J. Comput. Appl. Math.* 20(1):53–65. https://doi.org/10.1016/0377-0427(87)90125-7.

Nattapong Sanchan, Kalina Bontcheva, and Ahmet Aker. 2016. Understanding human preferences for summary designs in online debates domain. *Polibits* 54:79–85. https://doi.org/10.17562/PB-54-10.

Swapna Somasundaran and Janyce Wiebe. 2009. Recognizing stances in one debates. In *Proceedings of the Joint Conference of the 47th Annual Meeting of the ACL and the 4th International Joint Conference on Natural Language Processing of the AFNLP: Volume 1 - Volume 1*. Association for Computational Linguistics, Stroudsburg, PA, USA, ACL '09, pages 226–234. http://dl.acm.org/citation.cfm?id=1687878.1687912.

Shenghui Wang and Rob Koopman. 2017. Clustering articles based on semantic similarity. *Scientometrics* 111(2):1017–1031. https://doi.org/10.1007/s11192-017-2298-x.

ChengXiang Zhai, Atulya Velivelli, and Bei Yu. 2004. A cross-collection mixture model for comparative text mining. In *Proceedings of the Tenth ACM SIGKDD International Conference on Knowledge Discovery and Data Mining*. ACM, New York, NY, USA, KDD '04, pages 743–748. https://doi.org/10.1145/1014052.1014150.

A Game with a Purpose for Automatic Detection of Children's Speech Disabilities using Limited Speech Resources

Reem Elhady, Mohamed Elmahdy, Injy Hamed and **Slim Abdennadher**
German University in Cairo, Cairo, Egypt
Faculty of Media Engineering and Technology
reem.elhady@student.guc.edu.eg,
{mohamed.elmahdy,injy.hamed,slim.abdennadher}@guc.edu.eg

Abstract

Speech therapists and researchers are becoming more concerned with the use of computer-based systems in the therapy of speech disorders. In this paper, we propose a computer-based game with a purpose (GWAP) for speech therapy of Egyptian speaking children suffering from Dyslalia. Our aim is to detect if a certain phoneme is pronounced correctly. An Egyptian Arabic speech corpus has been collected. A baseline acoustic model was trained using the Egyptian corpus. In order to benefit from existing large amounts of Modern Standard Arabic (MSA) resources, MSA acoustic models were adapted with the collected Egyptian corpus. An independent testing set that covers common speech disorders has been collected for Egyptian speakers. Results show that adapted acoustic models give better recognition accuracy which could be relied on in the game and that children show more interest in playing the game than in visiting the therapist. A noticeable progress in children Dyslalia appeared with the proposed system.

1 Introduction

Speech and language disorders can affect a persons ability to talk, understand, read, write and express himself/herself. In this study, we are concerned with Dyslalia speech disorder. Dyslalia is an articulatory disorder in which children, or adults, do not pronounce the sounds clearly, sounds are changed or distorted or they replace one sound for another, e.g. a person may have a lisp use of the /T/ instead of the /s/ sound[1]. It is a result of having the sound pronounced from an incorrect part of the vocal tract. It may be also due to delayed speech, hearing impairment or learning disability. Mental retardation can also cause Dyslalia.

In the process of therapy, speech therapists use a variety of strategies including oral motor therapy, articulation therapy, and language intervention activities. In the step of oral motor therapy, the therapist uses a variety of oral exercises, including facial massage and various tongue, lip, and jaw exercises, to strengthen the muscles of the mouth. The therapists physically show the child how to make certain sounds, such as the /r/ sound, and may demonstrate how to move the tongue to produce specific sounds. During the language intervention activities, the therapist interacts with a child by playing and talking. They may use pictures, books, objects, or ongoing events to stimulate language development. The therapist may also model correct pronunciation and use repetition exercises to build speech and language skills.

Our proposed system plays the role of language intervention activities. Therapists not only have to

[1]Throughout the paper, SAMPA notation is used for phonetic transcriptions (Wells, 2002).

Proceedings of Natural Language Processing and Information Retrieval Workshop, pages 28–34,
Varna, Bulgaria, Sep 7 2017.

provide a variety of materials for different tasks for each therapy session, but they also have to keep a record of the childs performance during the tasks. Moreover, the therapist usually has problems to manage the recording details of these sessions for further analysis and to prepare appropriate materials that address the required treatment process.

Several studies mention the importance of computer-based systems that aim at supporting such therapies (Murray and Parker, 2004; Cagatay et al., 2012; Tobolcea and Danubianu, 2010). All of these studies have focused on Latin languages like English and Romanian.

There were specific criteria chosen in the proposed game design (Koster, 2013) for best effect: attractiveness, curiosity, immediate and accurate feedback, the issue of control, challenge feeling, and automatic system adaptation to user's performance. The experiments were done on the most common problems in the Arabic Egyptian language which are the replacement of the (س) /s/ phoneme to (ش) /S/, (ث) /T/, (د) /d/, or (خ) /x/ ;and the replacement of (ر) /r/ phoneme to (ل) /l/, (ي) /i:/ , or (غ) /G/ (Danubianu et al., 2009; Kotby M, 1979).

2 Speech Engine

In order to have a game that improves child Dyslalia, there should be first a speech engine that can accurately and automatically detect the problem in the child pronunciation, then the game shall take its role. So, we have worked separately on speech engine, and after we had successfully ensured recognition accuracy of the engine, we have merged it to an attractive game to test the effect of the game therapeutically. A major problem in Arabic speech recognition is the existence of quite many different Arabic dialects. Every country has its own dialect and sometimes there exist different dialects within the same country. There are many speech data resources for MSA, but unfortunately, the available resources for dialectal Arabic are very limited. That is why there are only limited researches done in the area of dialectal Arabic speech recognition. In this paper, we are proposing a cross-lingual acoustic modeling approach for dialectal Arabic, where we can benefit from existing MSA speech resources, in order to improve dialectal Egyptian Arabic recognition rate.

2.1 Speech corpora

2.1.1 MSA corpus

The existing MSA speech resource we used is the Nemlar news broadcast speech corpus. It was chosen in training MSA acoustic models (Yaseen et al., 2006). The corpus consists of 33 hours of MSA news broadcast speech. The broadcasts were recorded from different radio stations. All files were recorded in linear PCM format, 16 kHz, and 16 bit. The total number of speakers is 259 and the lexicon size is 62K distinct words with a phoneme set of 34 phonemes. This corpus was mainly selected because the transcriptions are fully vowelized and manually reviewed, and hence there were accurate phonetic transcriptions. The Nemlar corpus excluded speech segments with music or noise in the background. Cross-talks and segments with truncated words were excluded as well.

2.1.2 Egyptian Arabic Corpus

In order to adapt MSA and make it Egyptian dialect dependent and hence improve the recognition rate, we have used a previously collected Egyptian corpus (Elmahdy et al., 2010); a database of most frequently used words and utterances. The database includes utterances from different speech domains like greetings, time and dates, words spelling, restaurants, train reservation, Egyptian proverbs, etc. The diversity of speech domains ensures good coverage of acoustic features. A lexicon of 700 words was used with accurate phonetic transcription using the dictionaries (Hinds and Badawi, 2009) and (Stevens and Maurice, 2005). The total number of speakers is 22 native Egyptian speakers with tri-phones coverage of 15K distinct tri-phones. Every speaker was prompted to read 50 utterances chosen randomly from the database. All recordings were performed in linear PCM, 16 kHz, and 16 bits. The Egyptian corpus was used as a training set to train the Egyptian baseline acoustic model and in adapting existing MSA acoustic model.

2.1.3 Experimental Testing Corpus

Since the main objective is to test if the implemented engine detects the defected phonemes or not, subjects for this experiment were adults and children. This was intended to make sure that the engine works generic on all people suffering from Dyslalia not only children. We had ten subjects, six adults; three males and three females, and four children; three girls and one boy, aged from 7 to 10 years old.

Subjects were males and females who responded to a general request for participation in an Automatic Speech Recognition experiment. All subjects were normal people without any speech problem diagnosed. There were no any age or gender restrictions. The reason why the chosen subjects were not suffering from dyslalia, is the difficulty of exactly identifying the wrong phoneme pronunciation since the patient may have a problem in more than one phoneme in the word. Our strategy was to test specific phoneme each time, so that would have given us wrong indication.

The tool being used for speech collection is Audacity; a free audio editor and recorder. The recording was in a closed room free from any noise. Subjects used a Microsoft LifeChat LX-3000 microphone while recording for better and clear audio files. Files are recorded in PCM, mono channel, and sampling frequency of 16 kHz. Each subject was asked to record specific words that consist of the (س) /s/ and (ر) /r/ phonemes, where the phoneme is placed in the beginning, middle and ending of the word. The subjects were asked to record each of these words several times, but with a replacement of the correct phoneme to its Dyslalia replacements. These were the data that have been used for testing recognition accuracy. Each of the collected recorded words was associated with the actual phonetic transcription and the expected correct phonetic transcription. This allows us to identify whether the word is pronounced correctly, or the Dyslalia replacement in case of wrong pronunciation. An example from the collected testing set is shown in Table 1 where the two words سماعه and بسكويت are pronounced correctly with the /s/ phoneme (/sma?:h/ and /bskawi:t/ respectively), and all common Dyslalia replacements with phonemes /S/, /T/, /d/, and /x/.

2.2 Adaptation and Results

The whole amount of the MSA corpus was used to train the MSA acoustic model with a typical number of tied-states and Gaussians of 3,000 and 8 respectively. The MSA acoustic model has been adapted in order to make it dialect-dependent and hence improve the recognition rate. The MSA acoustic model was adapted using the Egyptian training set along with the normalized transcriptions. CMU Sphinx has been used in this work (Elmahdy et al., 2012). Below are the three adaptation techniques that were evaluated. In all the adaptation techniques, we compared word recognition accuracy, phoneme recognition accuracy, and their normalization recognition accuracy. This comparison is calculated using the process of force-alignment which takes an existing transcript and finds out which, among the many pronunciations for the words, or each phoneme in the word occurring in the transcript, are the correct pronunciations. For the phoneme, the output is written into a file with .phsegdir file name extension in sphinx3_align and it contains each phone start and end positions in terms of frames on time scale (100 frames per second) along with the log likelihood acoustic spectral match score. For the whole word, the output is written into a file with .wdsegdir file name extension in sphinx3_align and it contains also the word start and end positions in terms of frames on time scale along with large negative acoustic spectral match score. For the normalization, the match score of the targeted phoneme is divided by the match score of the whole word. We have used Confusion Matrix (CM) method for Word, Phoneme and their normalization as well in testing the results. The idea in the three scenarios is that we get the final match score; e.g. the Phoneme CM, for each word tested, we get the score of the phoneme we want to test with its correct audio reference and start to compare it with other known defects of this phoneme. The lowest score in a row is the best match, and hence the replaced phoneme is detected. Table 2 shows a sample of phoneme CM confidence scores where the word is detected as correctly pronounced if the largest log likelihood value is on the diagonal.

Correct	سماعه	بسكويت
س /s/	/sma?:h/	/bskawi:t/
ش /S/	/Sma?:h/	/bSkawi:t/
ث /T/	/Tma?:h/	/bTkawi:t/
د /d/	/dma?:h/	/bdkawi:t/
خ /x/	/xma?:h/	/bxkawi:t/

Table 1: Sample from the subjects' experiment for the Phoneme (س) with all possible Dyslalia replacements

2.2.1 Maximum A-Posteriori (MAP) Adaptation

As shown in Tables 3 and 4, the MAP adapted model resulted in 86.2% recognition accuracy in case of (س) /s/ phoneme-based CM acoustic modeling, and 83.1% recognition accuracy in case of (ر) /r/ phoneme-based CM acoustic modeling, which are actually worse than the baseline with 3% and 4% absolute. This result was almost predictable since MAP adaptation requires large data set for adaptation which was not the case in this experiment.

2.2.2 Maximum Likelihood Linear Regression (MLLR) Adaptation

As shown in Tables 3 and 4, MLLR adaptation was found to give better results when adapting all acoustic model parameters: Gaussian means, variances, mixture weights, and transition weights. In the case of phoneme-based CM acoustic modeling, the adapted MSA model performed recognition accuracy of 92.3% in case of (س) /s/, and 91.2% in case of (ر) /r/ which are actually better than the baseline with 3% and 4% absolute.

2.2.3 Combined MAP & MLLR Adaptation

The combination of MAP and MLLR resulted in the best recognition accuracy As shown in Tables 3 and 4. In the case of phoneme-based CM acoustic modeling, the adapted MSA model performed recognition accuracy of 93.4% in case of (س) /s/ as shown in Table 3, and 95.6% in case of (ر) /r/ as shown in Table 4 which are actually 4% and 8% absolute increase compared to the baseline.

3 "Kalemni Aktar"

"Kalemni Aktar" ("Talk to me more") is our proposed web GWAP that is used mainly to help Dyslalia children improve their Dyslalia. It also works as a tool for therapists to monitor their patients progress.

3.1 Game Design

"Kalemni Aktar" is a web game application; it is either a one player game or a two player game for the sake of competition. There are three main interfaces; Player, Physician, Admin. The game is divided into three rounds. In the player interface, once the player is logged in and the game starts, he/she chooses a theme to continue the game with

Figure 1: *Kalemni Aktar* ("Talk to me more") GWAP graphical user interface

by selecting between the following: Zoo, Kitchen, or Around the world. In the 1st round of the game, the player is directed to all the Arabic Phonemes to pick a phoneme out of the Arabic 28 phonemes. A round of random three words with the selected phoneme on the beginning, middle, and end appear to the player in bubbles. The player must click on the 3 bubbles but in any order he/she wants, to explode with an image, text, and a stored audio of the target word. For each round, there is a timer of 180 seconds set. This is done to increase the challenge for the players. Within this interval of time, it is possible to have 5 trials for each word. For each trial, the system detects if the phoneme in the word is pronounced correctly or not. If it is correct, the system automatically moves to the next word in the round, else the system recognizes the said word as a feedback to the player to help him in the other 4 trials. In Fig. 1 the player should have said سمكة /smkh/ (word appearing in green color), but the player said ثمكة /Tmkh/ (word appearing in red color) instead.

Since one of the incentives in GWAPs that engage and motivate players is the score (Von, 2006). The score for each round is calculated as follows:

- If the word is pronounced correctly from the first trial, the player gets 10 Points.
- If the word is pronounced correctly from the second trial, the player gets only 8 points.
- If the word is pronounced correctly from the third trial, the player gets only 6 points.

Table 2: Sample for phoneme confusion matrix confidence score.

Audio-Text	سماعه /sma?:h/	شماعه /Sma?:h/	ثماعه /Tma?:h/	دماعه /dma?:h/	خماعه /xma?:h/
سماعه /sma?:h/	-2269102	-2514996	-2327558	-2453191	-2482886
شماعه /Sma?:h/	-2427326	-2319749	-4686261	-2399874	-2325771
ثماعه /Tma?:h/	-2262885	-2322751	-2222441	-2263326	-2266508
دماعه /dma?:h/	-2310795	-2370847	-2233933	-2231769	-2278456
خماعه /xma?:h/	-2247120	-2301651	-2480661	-2224442	-2110647

Table 3: Recognition accuracy (%) for the different adaptation techniques for (س) /s/ phoneme CM results of the subjects' collected data.

Technique	Phone	Word	Norm.
Baseline	89.2	86.1	90.4
MAP	86.2	82.1	88.1
MLLR	92.3	86.1	92.3
MAP + MLLR	93.4	89.6	92.4

Table 4: Recognition accuracy (%) for the different adaptation Techniques for (ر) /r/ Phoneme CM results of the subjects' collected data.

Technique	Phone	Word	Norm.
Baseline	87.1	86.3	86.2
MAP	83.1	82.2	83.2
MLLR	91.2	89.1	89.4
MAP + MLLR	95.6	93.1	94.2

- If the word is pronounced correctly from the fourth trial, the player gets only 4 points.
- If the word is pronounced correctly from the fifth trial, the player gets only 2 points.
- Finally, if after the 5 trials the player still pronounces the word incorrect, he/she does not achieve any point.

After each round, a feedback appears to the player with the achieved score. This is repeated till all phonemes are pronounced. At the end of this level, a summarized report appears to the player with the feedback of the detected phoneme problems of all phoneme rounds. The 2nd round is the automatic system adaptation to the performance in the 1st level. It consists of some exercises with random words on those detected phoneme issues. The 3rd round is a tongue twister, a proficiency level stressing on certain phoneme which evaluates several words at the same time. In the physician Interface, speech therapists have access to their patients profiles to monitor the progress of the cases they have; so that they can assist in the sessions. For the Admin Interface, it is a basic interface for managing game content. By going through the game, all proven important game design factors from attractiveness, curiosity, immediate and accurate feedback, the issue of control, challenge feeling, and automatic system adaptation to user performance were covered (Umanski et al., 2008).

3.2 Subjects and Experiment

Subjects for this game were twenty children; ten boys, and ten girls aged from seven years old to ten years old. They are patients in Ain Shams Specialized Hospital. The subjects were chosen suffering from same level of Dyslalia specifically from the phonemes (س) /s/ and (ر) /r/. The twenty children were not able to pronounce the targeted phoneme correctly. Subjects were divided into two groups; each group consists of five boys, and five girls. The 1st group was having basic normal sessions with the speech therapist. The 2nd group was introduced to the implemented game in the session. The sessions were held for thirty to sixty minutes twice a week. The duration of the experiment was two months. The experiment had two main targets. The 1st target was to detect the accuracy of the game to see whether it could be really relied on for detecting the defected phonemes with its wrong replacement or not. The 2nd target was to compare the progress of the child speech when playing the game than when having normal sessions with the speech therapist. Throughout the two months experiments, the subjects of the two groups were monitored and interviewed about their feedback, level of interest and motivation.

3.3 Experimental Results

All subjects were introduced to a new speech therapist, who hasn't been involved earlier in the experiment, to test the children's level of dyslalia in the targeted phonemes after the two months therapy. This was to make sure that results will be double blinded. After gathering all test results for the two groups, results showed that both groups were been able to develop the (س) /s/ and (ر) /r/ phonemes better compared to the beginning of the experiment; however the 2nd group determine faster progress in speech than the 1st group does.

For the phoneme (س) /s/, nine out of the ten children of the second group were able to pronounce the (س) /s/ correctly, however one child still pronounces (ث) /T/ instead. In comparison to the first group where only seven out of the ten children were able to pronounce it correctly as shown in Fig. 2. For the phoneme (ر) /r/ , nine out of the ten children of the second group were able to pronounce the (ر) /r/ correctly, however one child pronounced (ي) /?:/ instead. In comparison to the first group where only six out of the ten were able to pronounce it correctly as shown in Fig. 3.

The children in the second group reported very good feedback, they were interested in using the application and switching between different themes, and phonemes. They found the interfaces friendly with suitable colors, and the characters of the game attracted their attention. Some mentioned that they were very curious to explore the different levels, and to achieve the highest score possible. While the children in the 1st group reported quite negative feedback compared to the others, some mentioned that they got bored in the therapy, some wanted to return home, and some got unmotivated throughout the session.

The use of such computer-based methods during various phases of the speech therapy determines a new psychological and pedagogical situation by creating a special interesting learning environment, and by facilitating a new, superior method for correcting and developing speech.

4 Conclusion and Future Work

We have presented a speech recognition based system for Dyslalia children called Kalemni Aktar. The aim is to provide assistance to Dyslalia children to improve their speech. Results showed

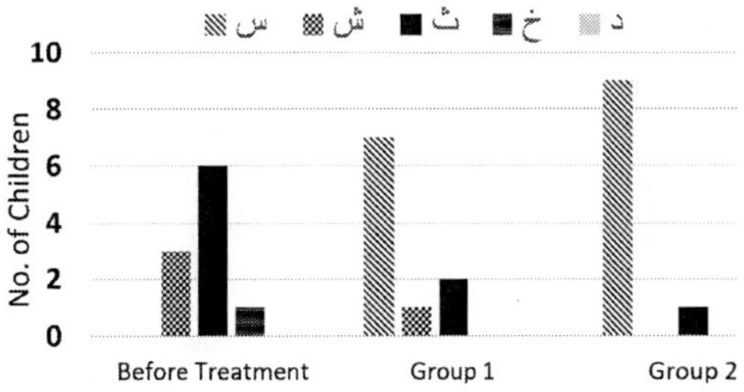

Figure 2: The progress after two months for phoneme (س) /s/

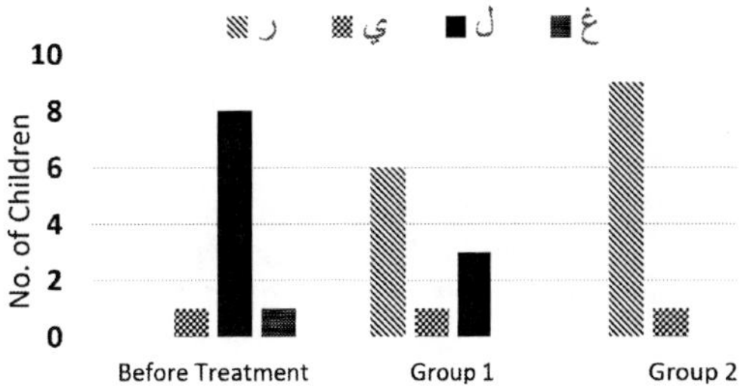

Figure 3: The progress after two months for phoneme (ر) /r/

that Kalemni Aktar reached its goal of providing a suitable and useful environment for the Dyslalia child to develop his/her speech. It has been shown that MAP + MLLR combined adaptation technique has best recognition results with accuracy reached 93.4% for (س) /s/ phoneme and 95.6% for (ر) /r/ phoneme.

"Kalemni Aktar" turned out to be a real help in the therapeutic activity, by providing various exercises that children can do both in the sessions and at home. Computer games are a powerful tool for motivating children to practice speech motor skills. The existence of computer based methods cannot replace the therapists role, but it only helps them in the therapy and helps the children having more exercises at home to develop their speech. The experiments showed high attention and concentration levels of children who practiced, as well as improvement in performance in terms of the game scores. The visual environments used in the prototype game proved to be easy for children to relate to, however more variety is needed to sustain curiosity.

For future work, we recommend upgrading the application by including all other Dyslalia types. The game may also include detection of other speech problems as stuttering to be fully integrated software for all speech disorders. It is also important to evaluate the application by involving more Dyslalia children in the testing phase, this will help to adapt the application according to their assessed needs. This Game can be of great importance to some nonprofit organizations in the sake of improving the society.

References

Mehmet Cagatay, Pinar Ege, Gul Tokdemir, and Nergiz Ercil Cagiltay. 2012. A serious game for speech disorder children therapy. In *7th International IEEE Symposium on Health Informatics and Bioinformatics (HIBIT)*. pages 18–23.

Mirela Danubianu, Stefan gheorghe Pentiuc, Ovidiu Andrei, Schipor Marian, Nestor Ioan, Ungureanu Doina, and Maria Schipor. 2009. Terapers- intelligent solution for personalized therapy of speech disorders .

Mohamed Elmahdy, Rainer Gruhn, and Wolfgang Minker. 2012. *Novel techniques for dialectal Arabic speech recognition*. Springer Science & Business Media.

Mohamed Elmahdy, Rainer Gruhn, Wolfgang Minker, and Slim Abdennadher. 2010. Cross-lingual acoustic modeling for dialectal Arabic speech recognition. In *INTERSPEECH*. pages 873–876.

Martin Hinds and El-Said Badawi. 2009. *A Dictionary of Egyptian Arabic*. Librairie du Liban.

Raph Koster. 2013. *Theory of fun for game design*. O'Reilly Media, Inc.

N Barakah M Kotby M. 1979. Patterns of dyslalia in Egypt .

Tiffany G Murray and V Parker. 2004. Integration of computer-based technology into speech-language therapy. *Educational Technology* 31:53–59.

Stevens and Salib Maurice. 2005. *A Pocket Dictionary of the Spoken Arabic of Cairo*. The American University in Cairo Press, Second printing.

Iolanda Tobolcea and Mirela Danubianu. 2010. Computer-based programs in speech therapy of dyslalia and dyslexia-dysgraphia. *BRAIN. Broad Research in Artificial Intelligence and Neuroscience* 1(2):52–63.

Daniil Umanski, Walter A Kosters, Fons J Verbeek, and Niels O Schiller. 2008. Integrating computer games in speech therapy for children who stutter. In *First Workshop Child, Computer and Interaction (WOCCI)*. pages 17–21.

Ahn Von. 2006. Games with a purpose 39(6):92–94.

JC Wells. 2002. SAMPA for Arabic. www.phon.ucl.ac.uk/home/sampa/arabic.htm.

Mustafa Yaseen, M Attia, Bente Maegaard, Khalid Choukri, N Paulsson, S Haamid, Steven Krauwer, C Bendahman, Hanne Fersøe, M Rashwan, et al. 2006. Building annotated written and spoken arabic LRs in NEMLAR project. In *Proceedings of LREC*. pages 533–538.

Association for Computational Linguistics
209 N. Eighth Street
Stroudsburg, Pennsylvania 18360

CURRAN ASSOCIATES INC.
proceedings
.com

ISBN 978-1-5108-5524-3
9 781510 855243